Starting with story

Animal story activities

for early years

Lesley Clark

Author
Lesley Clark

Editors
Jane Bishop and Sally Gray

Assistant editor
Libby Russell

Series designer
Joy White

Illustrations
Clare Boyce (Graham-Cameron Illustration)

Cover
Sarah Laver

Designed using Aldus Pagemaker
Processed by Scholastic Ltd, Leamington Spa

Published by Scholastic Ltd, Villiers House, Clarendon Avenue,
Leamington Spa, Warwickshire CV32 5PR

© 1997 Scholastic Ltd Text © 1997 Lesley Clark
2 3 4 5 6 7 8 9   7 8 9 0 1 2 3 4 5

British Library Cataloguing-in-Publication Data
A catalogue record for this book is available from the British Library.

ISBN 0-590-53654-0

Contents

chapter four

The Three Billy Goats Gruff

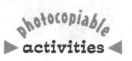

photocopiable activities

chapter five

The Town Mouse and the Country Mouse

Listening to and sharing stories is an important part of young children's learning which can deepen their understanding of the world they inhabit. Traditional stories offer young language learners the opportunity to actively participate in storytelling, to learn the structure of stories and to experiment with words and repetitive patterns and rhymes.

Young children also develop their listening and speaking skills in response to familiar and traditional tales. The framework of a traditional tale provides a basis for adding detail, changing or adapting endings and exploring moral messages.

The five stories within this book challenge the children to explore a range of emotions, helping them to confront their own fears and providing opportunities to talk about difficult issues such as bullying, loss of security and injustice.

Overall, this book aims to show how learning opportunities can derive from these popular stories in an interesting and informative way, presenting a flexible starting point for cross-curricular learning.

Getting ready for school

The activities in this book are designed for children who are working towards Key Stage 1 and tie in with the National Curriculum for Key Stage 1 and the Scottish Guidelines 5–14. Each chapter provides: two activities to cover English, two for mathematics and one each for science, design and technology, history, geography, art, music, PE and RE, as well as two on display and finally a cookery activity. The activities also link with the *Desirable Outcomes for Children's Learning* for five-year-olds identified by the School Curriculum and Assessment Authority, providing a suitable curriculum for playgroups, pre-school groups and nurseries, as well as for the children in reception classes.

How to use this book

Each chapter is based on a well-known story and provides a comprehensive range of activities and supporting material from which a topic-based approach to learning can be developed.

The format for each activity is the same with a learning objective, group size, details of things you will need and any necessary preparation listed. The ideal group sizes listed at the start of each activity reflect a belief that close adult support and conversation are fundamental to quality early years education. The activity itself is described and any useful discussion areas are then highlighted. Ways to support younger children and ideas to extend older children are provided as well as follow-up activities which offer both ways of enriching and ways of developing the original activity.

When undertaking any cookery activity, it is essential that you establish a regular hygiene routine. Before you begin make sure all children wear a protective apron and wash their hands thoroughly. Be sensitive to individual children's cultural or religious customs, and practices such as vegetarianism which will limit the consumption of some foods. Ensure that you are aware of any food allergies, intolerances or special dietary requirements and that all relevant information is documented for other staff.

At the back of the book there are ten photocopiable pages, two per chapter which each relate specifically to one of the main activities or one of the follow-up suggestions.

Practical activities

There are many ways of using this book which has been designed to suit the needs of early years' practitioners. You could follow through the chapter in sequence or choose activities randomly to provide a rich and varied range of practical tasks. You may wish to select one particular story which has specific appeal, as each chapter has been constructed to be free-standing and used independently. The whole programme can be covered from beginning to end or dipped into over a longer period of time, or revisited from year to year, without direct repetition. This should be useful for those settings with mixed-aged children who need to devise a form of rolling programme in their planning.

Although it is not essential to cover each activity in any chapter, following the whole schedule will give a well-balanced programme of practical and imaginative activities, covering all areas of the curriculum. This should enable young children to explore a wide range of appropriate, stimulating and enjoyable activities which are related to the magical world of well-loved animal fairy stories.

Links with home

The shared nature of well-known traditional tales makes them an ideal way to develop good links between your setting and the children's homes. Many of the children's families will have their own versions of the tales, all of which are relevant and enrich the children's understanding. Invite parents and carers to come in and tell their own versions of the tales, or other traditional tales from the varying backgrounds and cultural traditions of the children's homes. These stories spill over from one generation to the next, their familiarity makes it easier to invent games, role-play and other practical activities.

Finally, don't forget to invite parents, grandparents and carers into your setting to see the work that the children have been doing. This is a perfect opportunity to share their versions of traditional stories with the children and to talk about what their own school days were like.

chapter one
▶ introduction ◀

The Three Little Pigs

The Three Little Pigs is a classic tale which offers plenty of scope for considering our homes, our local environment, construction, feeling safe... and of course, pigs! There are other challenges too in its strong sense of good and evil, of learning to do things independently and in taking responsibility.

Once upon a time three little pigs lived in a tiny cottage with their Mother. They grew and grew, until one day their Mother sighed 'You boys will have to go and build your own homes'.

The little pigs set off. They hadn't gone far when they met a man carrying straw on his cart. The first little pig swapped his lunch for the straw and set about making his home. His brothers continued down the lane, where they met a young girl carrying sticks. 'I'll swap you those for my drink,' said the second little pig and he started building his house at once. Around the corner, the third little pig stopped a lorry laden with bricks and offered the driver his fine jacket in exchange for them. He too was now ready to build a home.

A week later, the first little pig was in his new home when a big shadow fell across the lawn. It was a huge, hungry wolf. Little pig fled inside, locking the door and diving under his bed. The wolf peered through the window and shouted, 'Little pig, little pig let me in!' 'Not by the hair on my chinny chin chin,' replied the pig. The wolf laughed and muttered, 'Then I'll huff and I'll puff and I'll blow your house down'. And he blew the house down flatter than a straw hat. The little pig just managed to wriggle free and dashed to his brother's house of sticks. They both hid under the table as the wolf peered between the wooden planks shouting, 'Little pigs, little pigs let me in!' They replied, 'No, no, not by the hairs on our chinny chin chins'. 'Well,' sighed the wolf 'I'll huff and I'll puff and I'll blow your house down!' And he did, scattering the sticks all around. The two pigs ran to the last little pig's brick house.

The wolf was close behind, so they shut the door and locked it. Again the wolf called out, 'Little pigs, little pigs, let me in!' 'No, no, no, not by the hairs on our chinny chin chins,' they replied. So the wolf yelled, 'Then I'll huff and I'll puff and I'll blow your house down!' So he huffed and he puffed...and he huffed and he puffed, but still the house didn't blow down. The wolf had just enough energy to crawl home. He decided to give up eating pigs because they were too much trouble.

The pigs danced for joy and ate a huge tea. Next day they started building an extension (made from bricks of course) so they could *all* live happily together.

Building with sounds

Objective
English – to develop recognition of initial letter sounds.

Group size
Whole group, then up to eight children.

What you need
Duplo size bricks, small pieces of card and scraps of paper, three large sheets of card, range of colourful writing tools, scissors, Blu-Tack, adhesive, white board/chalkboard.

Preparation
On each of the three large sheets, draw an outline of a different style of house. Cut up examples of appropriately sized paper bricks, sticks and straw. Write out examples of initial letter sounds 'p', 'w' and 'l', together with a paper brick, stick and piece of straw with the words 'pig, 'wolf' and 'little' on them.

What to do
Explain that you're going to play a listening game, building three different letter-houses containing words which all start with the same sound.

Say the words 'pig' 'wolf' and 'little' very clearly, repeating as you write each on a board. Repeat, this time only writing the first letter. Now match the letter to the word and ask the children to do the same with your paper bricks. Collect examples of names and objects which begin with each letter sound and practise saying these with the children.

Divide the children into three letter-house groups. Help the children to trace round or draw their own big paper sticks and bricks. Work co-operatively to fill each child's brick with an appropriate word, encouraging the children to come up with several words beginning with that letter.

Stick onto the house, decorate and read back to the whole group.

Discussion
Explain the meaning of terms such as letter and word. Explain that each letter makes a different sound and ask: what sound can you hear at the start of your name? What sound can you hear at the start of 'pig'? Praise the children's attempts and controlled listening skills. Using multisensory methods focus on and describe the shape and formation of each letter. Ask: where do we start that letter? What shape do we make? Look at each word and ask the children to say which is the longest/shortest word.

For younger children
Emphasise the tactile feel of each letter by using giant tactile letters for the children to trace over. Encourage the children to reproduce the shape using finger paints as they say the letter sound.

For older children
Focus on understanding the sound-symbol match and making a distinction between letters and words. Encourage the children to produce a flowing pattern with the letter shape.

Follow-up activities
▲ Emphasise the visual differences between words by cutting out contoured word bricks and then matching each up with a silhouette.
▲ Make giant letter collages using construction equipment and materials.

Blow me down!

Objective
English – to describe change and to develop sequencing skills.

Group size
Six to eight children.

What you need
Book of the story with large clear pictures, A4 sized paper for each child, pens, pencils and crayons or sticky shapes and scissors, adhesive stick or stapler.

Preparation
Cut each A4 paper in half length-ways. Retell the story, encouraging the children to join in with the wolf and pig dialogue.

What to do
Show the children the book and talk about the pictures of the wolf about to blow a house down. Discuss what has changed in the next picture – the house is demolished, the pig is running away and the wolf is chasing him.

Ask half of the group to 'blow' and act like the wolf, while the others tremble, tumble down and run! Swap the roles over.

Give the children the two sheets of paper and explain that on the top piece they should draw the house standing with the wolf preparing to puff and on the second piece they should draw what happens next. Ask the children to keep the images clear by including the wolf and the house, in the same basic position on both pages. Leave a small margin down the left side. Finally, stick or staple the two pictures together (see below). Roll up the upper picture with a blunt pencil so that it can be flipped fast to create a moving image of change.

before   after

Discussion
Ask: what happened when the wolf arrived at little pig's house? What did the pig do? How would the wolf look? Talk to the children about things they can move by blowing. Consider what might 'blow' real houses down. Talk about feeling afraid and feeling safe.

For younger children
Limit the example to the house of straw, using bold yellow sticky-paper sticks to contrast with the dark crayoned wolf. Cut up and rearrange the sticks in pieces for the second picture.

For older children
The children can add speech bubbles and detail to their pictures, such as what happens to different parts of the house and to each pig. Felt-tipped pens and larger paper may be useful to keep the images clear.

Follow-up activities
▲ Teach the children the traditional 'Little pig, little pig...' refrain to encourage retelling.
▲ Ask the children to invent their own refrain for the wolf and the pigs.
▲ Print or paint a liquid house shape and then try to 'blow' the image with a straw.

Sort it out!

Objective
Mathematics – to develop sorting skills and comparative vocabulary.

Group size
Six to eight children, depending on materials.

What you need
Wide variety of toy construction equipment, different types of bricks, tiles, straw and sticks. Posters or pictures showing building sites or building materials.

Preparation
Arrange materials in an accessible way for your group of children to sort and share.

What to do
Discuss the three types of material used by the pigs to build their houses. Look at the building site pictures, noticing in particular different materials used. Help the children identify key materials, giving them time to examine the samples of bricks and tiles you have collected.

Explain that you want them to sort out the construction equipment so that it is in useful sets. Work with the children, showing them how the same types, sizes, shapes or colours of bricks could be chosen to do this, asking the children each time to define the groupings. After the children have had time to practise, allow them to sort a group of their own, limiting the materials to a manageable scale.

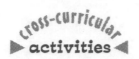

Discussion
Encourage understanding of the terms 'same and different' by manipulating a small range of real objects. Find identical sticks, some straw and two bricks and ask: Which are the same? How are they the same? Then ask the children to identify two things which are different, describing how. Ask: what do you do when you build/play and tidy your toys?

For younger children
Work closely with these children and limit the choice and range of equipment that they can use. This will help them to concentrate on the skill of sorting and should ensure that the children can sort successfully and define one or two attributes confidently.

For older children
Increase the range of materials so that they can be re-sorted in a variety of ways. Challenge them to explain the reasons for their sets of objects. Help establish which materials you have more of and which there are fewer of. Encourage the children to guess and count to confirm these comparisons.

Follow-up activities
▲ Use photocopiable page 87 to reinforce sorting and observational skills. Use the coloured-in pictures to make cards for snap and memory games.
▲ Explore the qualities of two- and three-dimensional shapes, so that children discover which fit together without leaving gaps, which roll and so on.
▲ Make patterns and structures using just three, four or five bricks/sticks. Make a display of them.

Pig tail measure up

Objective
Mathematics – to develop measuring skills and describe straight and curved shapes.

Group size
Six to eight children.

What you need
Differently coloured scraps of paper, pen, pencils, scissors and scraps of thick string, wool and card. Examples of straight and curved three-dimensional objects, simple rulers and measuring tapes.

Preparation
Draw differently sized circles on each scrap of paper, making two of similar size – draw wide concentric circles in pen as shown in the diagram below.

What to do
Ask the children if they can describe the shape of pigs' tails, reinforcing terms such as short, curly and round.

Show the children the circles and explain how they can cut along the lines, slowly turning the circle, to produce a pig's tail. Help each child cut around their circle to ensure success. When they have done this, compare each springy tail to find who has the longest and the shortest. Encourage guessing and visual comparisons by stretching out each tail, taking care not to break them.

Ask the children if they can see anything used for measuring. Demonstrate with a ruler and then with a tape. Which is easier? Show how the tape can be made curly or straight. Can the children think of ways they could compare the tails using something bendy? Have types of string, wool and card to experiment with.

Discussion
Focus on the differences between straight and curved using the three-dimensional objects. Introduce shape language by asking the children to feel an edge, corner, surface and so on. Name the measuring equipment and types of materials on display, drawing attention to their straight or bendy qualities. As the children are measuring, develop their comparative vocabulary, asking: which is long and which is short? Which tail is the shortest?

For younger children
Help with cutting, using wider circles and thicker paper for durability.

For older children
Encourage these children to explore the use of the tapes and rulers. Ask them to use suitable equipment to measure and order the different tails.

Follow-up activities
▲ Make curly tails out of different material to create mobiles.
▲ Make string pig tails and stick them onto card to create a printing block.
▲ Write a pig-tail tale around a giant circular spiral.

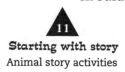

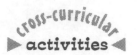

Lung power

Objective
Science – to explore the forces of blowing and sucking.

Group size
Six to eight children.

What you need
Range of lightweight objects: balloons, straws, paper, table tennis balls; and heavier objects: construction bricks, playing cards, sticks, golf balls. Cleaning materials.

Preparation
Clean the equipment and teach the children essential hygiene rules.

Practise making simple 'house' structures with cards, straw, sticks and bricks.

What to do
Ask the group how the wolf knocked the houses down and have fun re-enacting this part of the story. Select different 'wolves' to blow down a simple playing card house. Then substitute straw, sticks and finally bricks. Encourage the children to predict what will happen. Ask them what is making the straw move. What has happened to our wolf's puffing power? Use terms such as move/can't move and heavy/light.

Discuss the fact that blowing and sucking are opposite movements. Demonstrate for the children by blowing into a balloon so they can see it expanding, and sucking up a tissue with a straw. (Explain this is only safe for adults to do.)

Having discussed hygiene rules, let the children work in small groups with the materials of different weights. Invite the children to test out two contrasting objects in a blowing race.

Discussion
Observe and feel what happens as we breathe deeply in and out, ask: what happens to our cheeks/chests and mouths? What words can we use to describe blowing the balloon or sucking with a straw? Remind children of when they blow out candles, blow up armbands, suck drinks through straws, puff when running and so on.

For younger children
Keep the contrasts very simple and use hands to feel the force of sucking and blowing. Allow free experimentation and an emphasis on the sensation of blowing.

For older children
Focus more closely on what constitutes a fair test and how you measure the results.

Follow-up activities
▲ Use blowing to create paintings and scatter pictures.
▲ Explore what happens to our breathing as we exercise. How do we get puffed out?
▲ Develop empathy and understanding for those children with asthma.

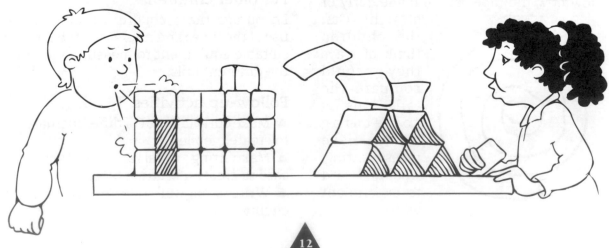

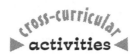
Perfect pigsty

Objective
Design and Technology – to design a pigsty.

Group size
Up to six children.

What you need
Toy pigs of various sizes, pictures of different types of real pig farms, junk cardboard boxes, tubes and pots, sticks and straw, soil, wood and construction bricks, adhesive, string, sticky tape, scissors, paper and pencils, board and marker or chalks.

Preparation
Ideally visit a pig farm or arrange for a pig and farmer to visit you! Cover surfaces and arrange the materials accessibly.

What to do
Use the farm pictures to prompt discussion about how real pigs live, and contrast this with the homes described in the story. What things do all homes have in common? Talk about what things a pig might need to feel safe and comfortable. Record key points visually on a board, such as a roof to keep dry, walls to feel safe, a door to get in and out, a bed for sleeping and so on.

Select a suitably sized toy pig and ask the group to design her a home. Examine and describe the range of materials and how things might be joined together. Help the children to sketch out their design first, then to look for appropriate materials. Allow them to try things out and offer practical support to ensure

success. Use soil and straw to line the floor and encourage the children to decorate their houses before each one is proudly displayed and described.

Discussion
Name the parts of houses and materials clearly. Talk about the similarities and differences between materials. Ask: why does a pig want a home? How can your house make a pig warm/safe/comfortable? Help the children to describe simply the shape, size and function of key parts of their design.

For younger children
Limit the materials provided and help the children to concentrate on the main parts of the house, such as floor, walls, roof and entrance.

For older children
Allow them to work independently and encourage them to review their work, suggesting and making improvements to their designs. Consider the function of different parts of the house and the strength of the structure.

Follow-up activities
▲ Compare and contrast human and animal homes, making a large frieze to illustrate this.
▲ Use model farms to encourage role-play.
▲ Make clay models of pigs and their homes.

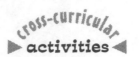 

History house walk

Objective
History – to compare different houses in the locality, noticing changes.

Group size
Whole group with the appropriate ratio of adult support.

What you need
Pictures and photographs of different building types, local reference material, samples of modern building materials and pictures of new houses. Clipboard, pencil, paper, 'checklist' and crayons for each child. Sketching materials, children's cameras, cassette recorder.

Preparation
Plan out a safe route which offeres a variety of buildings of different ages. Design a checklist of three to six features to distinguish such as chimney pots, brickwork, size of house/ flats, types of roofing, windows and doors. Decide in advance three contrasting houses and familiarise helpers with your learning objectives.

What to do
Remind the children of the three house types described in the story. Do they know of any houses using wood or straw in their locality? What types of houses are most commonly found? Show pictures of wooden huts, thatched cottages, castles and modern brick housing.

Explain that they are all going to be history detectives today, going on a walk to track down clues about how old different buildings might be. Talk them through the checklist carefully, agreeing how to tick or cross in the correct column and where to draw anything special about each part they are examining.

On the walk, allow plenty of time to feel surfaces, take rubbings, sketch, look for dates and unusual features on the buildings. On your return, make a pictorial record of key features you all found, and record the children's observations on tape, through sketches, photographs and so on.

Discussion
Ask the children to describe different parts of their homes, how they get in, how they see out, how they keep dry and so on. How do these features differ in different houses? Look for very new buildings and a much older house where the windows, roofing and doors are clearly different.

For younger children
Concentrate on two to three important features, on describing key parts of houses and on appreciating simple changes such as the size of windows and doors or the materials used.

For older children
Look in more depth for evidence of change and suggest basic reasons for this such as family size, new materials, machines and modern lifestyles.

Follow-up activities
▲ Create a simple house timeline, distinguishing which houses are older than the children and any that are younger.
▲ Create a 'History House' estate agents for others to visit.
▲ Arrange a trip to a nearby castle or local building site.

Pig's progress

Objective
Geography – to explore directions and to introduce simple maps.

Group size
Up to six children.

What you need
Simple large scale arrows and toy cars. A bench, three large hoops and a mat, paper, pens and pencils, chalk. Photocopiable page 88 for each child.

Preparation
Make your own large arrows. Arrange the room so that you can use the bench, hoops and mat as part of a creative journey to tell the story of the three pigs (see below). On appropriate flooring, draw a chalk 'road' linking these items. Copy this layout onto a plan to share with the children. Retell the story, emphasising each house and incident on the pigs' route.

What to do
Take your 'little pigs' on a journey like follow my leader around the apparatus. Talk them through the route as you go, inventing likely obstacles such as a long log bridge, three stepping stones to hop over

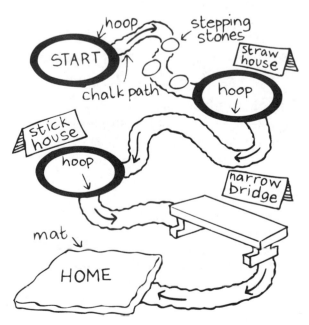

and a muddy puddle to roll in. (You are meant to be pigs!)

Show them your plan of the equipment. Let the children take turns in marking the route on the plan and being the leader, describing their chosen route. Relate each journey back to your map, marking the routes in differently coloured pens. Show the children your arrows and play matching games where they have to walk in the direction indicated.

Discuss the pigs' journey as outlined on photocopiable sheet 88. Locate the start of the journey, each house and the finish. Ask the children to mark on arrows and to draw details of what the pigs might encounter.

Discussion
Reinforce positional language by asking: what's in front of/behind/next to. Ask the children what arrows are for and how they show us which direction to go. Explore different ways of turning and moving so the children can respond to forwards/backwards/sideways movements. Compare and contrast familiar routine journeys around the room or building to reinforce the concept.

For younger children
Use directional arrows and language to describe straight or curved sections of the route. Let them draw on their own details.

For older children
Encourage the children to devise further symbols for their story map.

Follow-up activities
▲ Make simple picture maps of your room, or a model of your grounds outside.
▲ Point to the story map as the children enact the story sequence.
▲ Collect environmental signs and symbols, scoring points like 'I spy' booklets depending on how easy they are to spot.

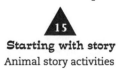

Piggy printing

Objective
Art – to explore a range of printing effects.

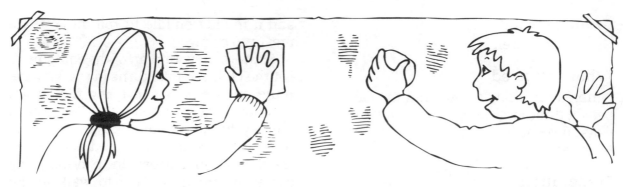

Group size
Up to six children.

What you need
Thick paint in bold primary colours, four trays or shallow tins, scrap paper and strips of white and black paper, a few construction pieces suitable for printing, potato, sharp knife, string, twigs, hay, bricks, tiles, cardboard blocks, scissors, adhesive, space for drying, bowl of soapy water, cleaning equipment.

Preparation
Make four contrasting prints (one of each colour), one with Sticklebricks, one with a twig, one using hay and one from the side of a tile. Make one print block by winding string into a pig's tail shape and gluing it onto a cardboard block. Make one pig's trotter-shaped potato cutting.

What to do
Show the children your four prints and ask them to describe the colours and shapes they see. Look at the items you used and match each to its print, describing the different effects they made.

Demonstrate different printing techniques such as submerging and removing the object from a film of thick paint then pressing your paper evenly over the top or painting the object and printing by pressing one side onto paper before carefully lifting off. Show the pig's tail block and the potato trotters and invite the children to count and observe as you produce a repeating pattern along a strip of paper.

Encourage the children to talk through their chosen printing method before taking their final prints, and to practise the correct pressure and handling it requires using scrap paper.

Discussion
Talk about the lines and shapes you see and how this is mirrored in the objects used for printing. Look for clues asking: which prints are large/have straight edges/have round patterns on? Ask which objects are easy to print with, which make clear shapes and which are muddled. What happens if you press too hard/too lightly?

For younger children
Use just one type of object and explore different printing techniques.

For older children
Experiment with applying different pressure as you print, with dragging the object slightly or with pressing it very lightly.

Follow-up activities
▲ Make designs with an odd one out or a pattern to detect.
▲ Use a simple print to introduce positional language and orientation, such as pigs with their tails printed in different positions.
▲ Print curtains, tablecloths and wallpaper for your little pig's home.

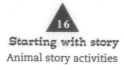

Huff puff music

Objective
Music – to explore the noises made by blowing and to look at wind instruments.

Group size
Whole group introduction, small groups of six children.

What you need
Plastic bottle, comb and paper, recordings of wind instruments (such as the bird, cat, duck and wolf in *Peter and the Wolf* by Prokofiev), non-pitched pipes, blowers, whistles, kazoos. Pictures or real examples of a recorder, oboe, clarinet, trumpet. Mild disinfectant and paper towels.

Preparation
Practice making noises on each item beforehand.

What to do
Remind the children of the wolf and his huffing and puffing. Turn the refrain ('I'll huff and I'll puff...') into an echoing game so that the children copy the speed or pitch of your voice. Ask a child to voice the wolf's part while you blow over a bottle top to produce a wind accompaniment. Repeat using other objects before progressing to using the musical instruments. Ask the children to close their eyes and to guess which object you use. Contrast blowing soft and hard, slow and fast, short and long. Let the children listen to the different wind instruments so they can discover their variety.

In a small group, ask one child to blow a tune with three to five contrasting beats, which another child tries to copy. Invite the rest of the group to describe

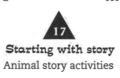

the tune and see whether the composer agrees! Now allow the children to experiment carefully at producing sounds with the different wind instruments. Ensure instruments are cleaned after every use.

Discussion
Ask the children whether your voice is high or low, loud or soft, fast or slow. Ask: how can we make sounds by blowing? Explore the sounds made by the objects and instruments, asking which sounds are easy to reproduce and how the children hold and control their blowing for each instrument.

For younger children
Let them experiment freely with two to three instruments, work with them to show them how to mirror sounds before they try to work with a partner.

For older children
Extend the range of instruments explored and help them to hear how the sounds might be varied in pitch and tone.

Follow-up activities
▲ Make a recording of the children's work. This could inspire artwork or be used to accompany retellings of the story.

▲ Invite musicians to perform, and include works from different times and cultures.

▲ Challenge the children to make wind instruments of their own by making available suitable materials.

Curly or straight?

Objective
PE – to explore contrasting body movements and ways of travelling.

Group size
Whole group.

What you need
Skipping ropes, one between two.

What to do
Begin with a gentle warm-up by asking the children to find a space and curl up tight, then slowly unfold and stretch out as straight as possible. Now ask the children to sit up straight choosing whether to have their legs bent or straight. Starting with fingers, slowly curl up and then stretch out, repeating with other body parts. From a standing position, ask the children to make careful circular motions with their arms and bodies.

Now let them experiment travelling as straight as possible or as curved as possible. Encourage them to listen carefully by asking them to prowl straight like a wolf when you puff and to move in a curvy way like a pig when you grunt.

Finally put the children in pairs and use the rope to focus on curved and straight motions. Start by making ropes as straight as possible and mirroring this with floor movements. Contrast by coiling the rope round and making curvy floor movements. Invite the children to take it in turns to position the rope and find ways of matching it. Share the children's ideas before winding down with a straight then curvy game of follow my leader.

Discussion
Ask: which parts of your body are curled tight? Which are hard to curl? How are you showing straight shapes? How can you balance and move keeping as curled as possible? Which ways of moving are easiest?

For younger children
Help them to work co-operatively and to describe movements accurately.

For older children
Having explored a range of contrasting movements, the children can work in pairs to develop a sequence of three to four movements for partners to describe and copy correctly.

Follow-up activities
▲ Find ways of travelling along a bench and of jumping in straight and more curved positions.
▲ Make up a curled dance and then a straight march.
▲ Examine straight and curved elements in performing a forward roll.

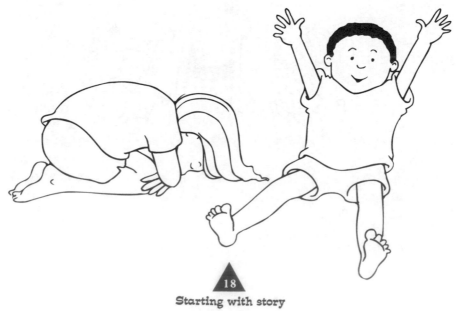

If a job's worth doing...

Objective
RE – to learn to celebrate achievement and effort.

Group size
Whole class, followed by groups of up to six children.

What you need
The story of the man who built his house upon the sand (Luke Chapter 6 v46-49) and the song 'The wise man and the foolish man' in *Okki-tokki-unga* (A&C Black), sandpit, dry sand, spades and building utensils, watering can, sticks, construction pieces, paper and drawing equipment.

Preparation
Fold the paper so as to provide four sequence pictures.

What to do
Ask the children whether the little pigs all built their houses in the same way and collect ideas about why the last little pig took so much longer. Explain that Jesus told a story about two men who each built a house, and tell or read the story to them. Ask for two volunteers to act out part of the story by building in the sandpit, one as quickly as possible using sand, the other carefully using construction bricks. After a few minutes ask the other children to judge who is in the lead. Then invite two volunteers to drop 'rain' on the two homes and to explain what happens.

Allow the children to experiment with the sand and building materials in small groups, asking them to build something very quickly and then something else very carefully. How did they feel each time about what they had made?

Remind them of the story and ask each child to produce two series of pictures (using both sides of the folded paper), one showing the wise man building carefully on the rocks and the other showing the foolish man building carelessly on the sand.

Discussion
Ask the children to talk about times when they have been careless, saying how they felt and what happened. Contrast this with times when they have taken great care over something. When is it particularly important to try our best? Ask: how do you feel when you've made a special birthday card or made a clever model?

For younger children
Concentrate on the joy of achieving something worthwhile, such as making a fantastic sand castle or doing brilliant pictures to retell the story.

For older children
The houses which took longer were much more difficult to build and had solid foundations. Help the children to compare this with their own achievements.

Follow-up activities
▲ Design posters to encourage others to tackle tasks with care and determination.
▲ Compile a pictorial collage showing occasions when care counts, such as making birthday cakes or getting dressed to go somewhere special.

Houses

What you need

Samples of bricks, building materials and wood, smooth large stones, straw, balsa scraps, cuboid junk boxes such as cereal packets and other cardboard boxes. Factory scraps including tubing and plastics. Table display space and storage boxes, backing paper (blue, brown, grey, brown, orange, green and yellow). Scissors, adhesive, large thick paper, paints, clear plastic pieces, collage materials and range of joining materials, books about houses.

Preparation

Put up backing paper for your three pig houses. Check all building materials for safety. Flatten straw. Ensure you have a good range of the same sized balsa scraps and cardboard boxes for collage construction. Cut thick paper to appropriate sizes for each house. Set up equipment into the three groupings. Sort and label construction material in the storage boxes.

What to do

Discuss each pig's home and look at some books and posters to gain ideas about different house shapes. Divide the children into three groups, to represent each of the three houses.

Ask the children to draw a house outline on the paper and encourage them to explore their collage materials and think about how they are going to be arranged and secured to the paper. Talk about the main features of a house and suggest these are painted or added to later. (The balsa and straw should be positioned carefully then stuck and left to dry before painting. The cuboid junk boxes will need to be sorted into different brick sizes before sticking and decorating.)

Secure to the backing board and design appropriate captions, perhaps using straw, stick or construction brick printing for the labels. Finally, arrange the construction material into the storage boxes and onto the tables. Set a weekly house-building challenge, using the floor space in front of your display.

Discussion

Talk about the variety of house types with which the children are familiar. Ask: why do we need homes? What do all homes have? Talk about the range of roofs, doors and windows and encourage a creative response in their own designs.

Follow-up activities

▲ Collect a gallery of pictures or photos showing the children's own houses, and find posters of unusual varieties.
▲ Use large bricks or blocks to make a house design outside.

Pigs

What you need

Backing paper, white paper, thick paints in white, red, yellow, blue, green, black. Variety of brushes, mixing palettes, sponges, combs. Buttons, small round tubs, newspaper, scissors, adhesive, straw, twigs, small amount of cement mix. Thick string of three different lengths. Posters and pictures of pigs.

Preparation

Put up backing paper and with the white paper, cut out and stick some cobble shapes to make a cobbled path for the pigs to walk down. Cut up white paper into three equal sizes and keep the scraps.

What to do

Explain to the children that they are going to do some colour mixing to make some 'pig' colours. Show the children how to drop paint from the pure colour tubs into their mixing palettes without getting the brushes dirty. Use another brush to mix and develop their own colours. After the children have had a chance to try out some colours, agree on three colours, one for each pig.

Help the children to draw pig outlines and then ask them to add their shades to the appropriate pig. Once each pig is covered, discuss whether they want to mark or blend the paint using the sponge, comb, fingers or thick dry brushes. Now decide how additional features – eyes, trotters, snout and tails are to be added and decorated. Discuss the shape, size and position of these features and secure them to your pigs.

Once the pigs are on the board (use scrumpled newspaper behind to pad your pigs slightly), let the children add clues so that each pig can be linked to a house. This can include scatterings of the building material and suitable tools for each pig to hold. Arrange each pig's tail in a curly pattern, so that the different lengths are clear. Let the children add clothing or hats if desired. Write out some labels asking about the colour of each pig and how it was made. Other labels could ask who has the longest tail, who made the house of bricks, who is on the right and who is in the middle.

Discussion

Ask the children to name each colour in the pots. Then ask them: which is the lightest? Which is the darkest? Talk about the features and characteristics of real pigs, and discuss times when the children have seen them.

Follow-up activities

▲ Make feely pig collages using contrasting collage materials.
▲ Make up poems related to pigs and for feelings/objects linked to your 'pig' colour.

Pig building biscuits

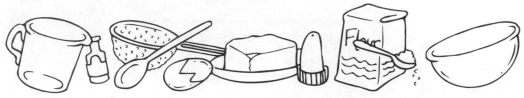

Group size

Up to six children.

What you need

Weighing scales, mixing bowls, jug or small bowl, wooden spoon, tablespoon, teaspoon, knife, fork, palette knife, sieve, rolling pins, baking trays, wire rack, plastic bag, cutters, aprons, refridgerator, washing and cleaning equipment. Ingredients: 200g self-raising flour, 125g butter/margarine, 100g sifted icing sugar, 1 egg, 6 drops vanilla essence, 1 teaspoon cinnamon, pinch of salt, currants, chopped cherries/dried apricots to decorate, milk if necessary. (Makes about 30.)

Preparation

Examine and weigh out ingredients with the children. Decide whether the children are going to make dough collectively or individually. If the latter, divide the ingredients up to avoid confusion.

What to do

Ensure the children understand hygiene rules. Preheat the oven at 180 °C (350 °F, Gas Mark 4). Help the children sift flour into the mixing bowl and add the salt and cinnamon. Cut the butter into tiny pieces and add to the flour. Now use fingertips to rub it together until there are no big lumps and it looks like bread crumbs. Make a deep well in the middle of the mixture. Meanwhile, whisk the egg (using the fork) in the jug, and count in the vanilla essence. Pour this down your well and use a spoon to start mixing. Knead the mixture with hands to make a stiff dough, adding a little milk if it's too dry. Roll into a big ball and place in the plastic bag. Leave this in the fridge while you wash up and clean surfaces.

Lightly flour the surfaces and give each child a lump of chilled dough to roll out. Let the children choose whether to use cutters, a rounded knife or to mould their own pig shapes. Explain that the pig needs to be quite thin if he is to cook properly. Press in eyes, ears, snouts and a tail if desired. Place well apart on greased baking trays and cook for 10 to 15 minutes until a pale golden brown colour. Cool on the wire racks whilst you clear up, before admiring and tasting!

Discussion

Talk through the weighing process, compare and contrast the ingredients. How does each change the other, and what colours, shapes, textures, tastes and smells do they detect while cooking? Use the experience to enrich language and observe changes accurately. Discuss hygiene and safety rules.

Follow-up activities

▲ Experiment by making your biscuits different flavours.
▲ Add pink water icing and other 'pig-style' decorations.

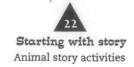

► introduction ◄

Goldilocks and The Three Bears

This tale has a delightful sense of adventure and naughtiness. Children share the suspense and enjoy the lovely musical quality of the refrains. The tale is also perfect for considering family roles and relationships as well as for extending language skills and numerical understanding. Here's a simple version to build on.

There was once a family of bears who loved porridge for breakfast. One morning the porridge smelled delicious but it was much too hot. 'I know,' said Daddy, 'let's go for a walk in the woods while it cools down'. So Mummy, Daddy and Baby bear set off.

Minutes later a little girl called Goldilocks passed by their cottage. She smelled the porridge and as she was very hungry, she peeped inside. Nobody at home! When she saw the three bowls of porridge she just had to try some. She dipped her finger in the biggest bowl, 'Too salty!' she cried. She tasted the next bowl, 'Horribly sweet!' But when she tasted the little bowl it was perfect, so she ate it all up.

Next, Goldilocks went to sit on a large old chair. 'Too hard!' she said. She tried a medium-sized chair but sunk down to the springs, 'Too soft!' she said. Then she spied a small wooden stool, which looked just right...until CRACK! She broke it to bits. Goldilocks trotted upstairs to find somewhere to rest. She saw three beds and flung herself on the largest. 'Oh!' she screamed. 'Hard as nails!' So she tried the medium-sized bed but that was soft as butter. Last of all she snuggled into the smallest bed and fell fast asleep.

Meanwhile, the three hungry bears returned to find the cottage door wide open. 'Who's been eating my porridge?' roared Daddy bear. 'Who's been eating my porridge?' asked Mummy bear. 'Who's been eating my porridge so *it's all gone*?' cried Baby bear, holding up his empty bowl. Just then, Daddy noticed a lump in his chair. 'Who's been sitting in my chair?' he bellowed. 'Who's been sitting in my chair?' echoed Mummy bear, and 'Who's been sitting on my stool and *broken it to bits?*' wailed Baby bear.

The bears dashed upstairs and Daddy Bear yelled, 'Who's been sleeping in my bed?' 'Who's been sleeping in my bed?' asked Mummy bear. But they both rushed over as Baby bear gave a shriek, 'Oooh! Who's been sleeping in my bed and LOOK *she's still there*!' The bears crowded around Goldilocks, giving her such a fright! She dashed past the bears out through the doors and disappeared into the woods. Of course, the bears never saw her again. As for them, they made some more porridge, mended the stool and felt much better!

Guess it Goldilocks!

Objective
English – to develop use of descriptive language and listening skills.

Group size
Whole group, then smaller groups of six.

What you need
Photocopiable page 89, card, coloured pencils.

Preparation
Photocopy page 89 onto card, ask the children to help colour the pictures very carefully, laminate if possible and cut out the cards. Play matching and sorting games with the cards so the children are familiar with them.

What to do
Tell the story, emphasising the parts of the story that are featured on the cards. Explain to the children that they are going to play a game where they have to listen carefully to clever clues, describing the object without saying what it is. Model this several times yourself, by showing one of the picture clues and then making up a short phrase to describe it. For example, saying, 'I'm big and soft and you lie in me to go to sleep'. Encourage the children to volunteer to have a go before breaking into smaller groups to play the game. Shuffle the cards and deal one to each player. Take turns to describe, the one who guesses first keeping the card. The game continues with each player taking a card from the top of the remaining pile, until all have been described.

Vary the activity to suit the needs of your group, always setting clear group rules for fairness and turn-taking.

Discussion
Start by helping the children to describe the object's size and shape. Think about where it's usually found and what it's made of. Ask: what do we use this for? Focus on listening skills – how do you show someone you are ready?; and on social skills – how shall we take turns and decide who can guess the answer?

For younger children
Use toy models so that the children can feel what they are describing and they can focus more easily on its colour and shape. Keep the clues in a large sack to play the guessing game.

For older children
Extend the range and quality of descriptive terms used, and find alternatives to the comparisons of size made in the story.

Follow-up activities
▲ Use the cards to play a memory game.
▲ Make a list of big, hard and sweet words to develop the children's vocabulary.
▲ Bring in a mystery object once a week to name and describe.

Golden rules for Goldilocks

Objective
English – to show how signs and symbols convey meaning.

Group size
The whole group, then groups of six to eight.

What you need
Examples of environmental signs and messages, shopping bags, highway code book, white board and red, green and black markers, pieces of card, colouring materials (limited to bold 'message' colours).

Preparation
Cut card into sign shapes so that each child has at least one. Produce three simple, large signs with picture symbols such as school children or a train, or important words like 'stop'. Plan your 'signs' walk.

What to do
Ask the children to retell what Goldilocks did in the story. Explore whether she was right or wrong and what 'rules' she was breaking. Explain that many rules are drawn as signs and that you're going on a hunt for some. (Use parking, entrance, toilet, fire and warning notices and so on.)

On your return, discuss the meaning of the three signs you have drawn, emphasising how important clear picture clues are. Refer back to Goldilocks to decide what sort of sign the bears could have on their front door. Help the children draw or write their own messages.

Discussion
Ask the children to look for signs and messages around houses and streets. Ask why they are short (such as 'Private!', 'Stop!' and 'No Entry!') or why pictures are often used. Ask: what signs can you read? Where do you see that sign and what is it for? Extend the discussion to symbols for services such as trains and telephones, and for shops and trucks.

For younger children
Give clear examples and draw useful picture clues such as Goldilocks 'crossed out' or an angry bear face. Help to write messages.

For older children
Encourage free writing and copying as children expand their knowledge of environmental symbols and words. Work with a partner to test whether signs are understood.

Follow-up activities
▲ Make a collection of local signs and symbols using photographs and large drawings. Ask the children to guess the location and purpose of each.
▲ Draw and write symbols and rules for your home corner area.
▲ Make up a short list of group rules.

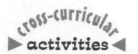

Pour the porridge

Objective

Mathematics – to encourage simple estimation and comparison of capacity.

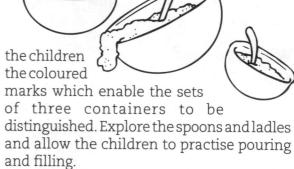

Group size

Up to six.

What you need

Sets of three differently sized clear plastic beakers, bottles and bowls, so that each child has at least one set to classify. Spoons and ladles, some the same size. Three identical tubs, water trough, aprons, cloth and mop, sticky labels, coloured pencils and crayons, marking pens.

Preparation

Mark containers within each set (for example, beakers) with a colour so that it can be clearly distinguished. Cut three sizes of sticky labels.

What to do

Examine the three identical beakers and ask the children if they are suitable for the bears. Explore some ways of testing the children's visual comparisons and establish that the beakers hold the same amount. Then take one set of non-identical beakers and ask the children to rank them, so that baby bear has the smallest and so on. Show the children the coloured marks which enable the sets of three containers to be distinguished. Explore the spoons and ladles and allow the children to practise pouring and filling.

Finally allocate each child a set of containers to classify. On a dry surface, ask them to use crayons to draw a picture of each bear on to the appropriately sized sticky label and then to stick the labels on to the matching sized containers.

Discussion

When comparing containers ask: which holds the most? Which holds the least? How can we find out whether this bowl holds more than that bowl? Describe the relative shape and size of different containers and ask: why is it easier to pour from the bottle than the bowl?

For younger children

Compare two containers and allow plenty of free experimentation. Help the children describe how full each is and show how the smaller can be emptied into the larger one.

For older children

Encourage counting and guessing as they experiment. How many times can Baby's beaker be emptied into Daddy's beaker?

Follow-up activities

▲ Prepare a display with sand, dry lentils, thick paint in little bottles to explore what is easy/hard to pour into trays.

▲ Use photocopiable page 89 to reinforce ordering skills. Invite the children to draw the three bears separately and assign them the appropriate cards.

Three in the family

Objective
Mathematics – to develop skills of making sets, counting and conservation of number.

Group size
A group of three or six children.

What you need
Three teddy bears, three sets of each – toy bowls, spoons (include one extra spoon), cups, bibs. Paper and felt-tipped pens, thick finger paint, shaving foam, sand and materials of different colours and textures. Table and three chairs. Sorting equipment such as Compare Bears (available from various educational suppliers).

Preparation
Make three large symbol 3's, using differently textured and coloured materials. Form a large 3 in the paint and take a print. Ensure the sorting equipment can be easily sorted into threes.

What to do
Ask the children how many bears were in the story. Show them the teddies and ask if there are enough. Count and name each bear before asking the children to count out one of each of the toy objects. Keep one of the small chairs back so that they need to establish that two is not enough, and that one more is needed (you have just mended baby bear's chair!). Now select three 'bear' volunteers and ask other children to lay a place setting for each. Establish that you have four spoons, one more than three and that this can be used to stir the porridge.

Show the children how to write a '3' and let them trace over your large textured samples, describing the movements they make. Explore with the foam and paint before taking prints of their own '3' formation. While their print is drying, use sorting equipment to make sets of three, and write labels underneath. Finally, encourage the children to draw three bears with three objects and to write the symbols '3' as a decorative border.

Discussion
Ask the children to count and establish the number sequence to three, finding out what is one more than/less than three. Ask them to find three bears and a spoon for each bear. How many spoons altogether? Count and move objects at the same time. Arrange three spoons differently.

For younger children
Reduce the number of examples and equipment. Emphasise multisensory formation.

For older children
Compare sets of different quantities below five, so as to establish number value and to increase confidence. Explore different ways of recording 'sets of three'. Write 3 in many different media.

Follow-up activities
▲ Produce a frieze showing famous '3' characters (pigs, goats and so on).
▲ Compare ages to find out who is three and who is older/younger than three.
▲ Make a giant three for a door display, sticking on sets of three objects.

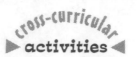

Feel it, taste it

Objective
Science – to learn how to use the senses to compare and contrast.

Group size
Up to six children.

What you need
Six different cereals in their packets (be aware of any children with allergies), bowl and spoon for each child, magnifying glasses, clear shallow dishes, tweezers, milk, pencils, paper, scarves, washing up and drying materials.

What to do
Ask the children what they eat for breakfast and count how many like the same thing as the bears. Remind the children why Goldilocks didn't like the first two bowls she tried and discuss how we taste things. Explain that they're going to test some cereals without looking at them first. (Stress the importance of following strict hygiene rules.) Blindfold each child with a scarf and give them a tiny amount of the same cereal to try. Ask them to feel it, smell it and then finally taste it, describing each experience, before trying to guess the name of the cereal. Make notes of what the children say. Remove blindfolds so they can see if they guessed right. Now repeat the exercise with a different cereal to try.

Use the comments that were made to play a guessing game with the other children. Finally, let them each choose a cereal to try, first dry, and then with milk, noting changes in appearance, texture and taste. Compare their findings and draw simple conclusions.

Discussion
Ask the children how they eat and taste, discuss our use of senses. Reinforce this by asking at each stage in the experiment: what does it feel/smell/sound/taste look like? Encourage the children to use descriptive terms such as sticky, lumpy and crunchy. Make comparisons between the cereals.

For younger children
Reduce the range of cereals so that strong contrasts may be drawn.

For older children
Ask older children to consider which sense they are isolating at each stage and encourage full, accurate comments. Use the tweezers and magnifying glasses to examine and draw individual pieces of cereal.

Follow-up activities
▲ Ask the children to design a packet cover or advert for their favourite breakfast cereal.

▲ Make a pictogram showing which cereal was the children's favourite.

▲ Use small amounts of cereal to create feely collage pictures.

A chair for Baby bear

Objective
Design and Technology – to make a simple seat.

Group size
Up to six children.

What you need
Soft toy bear, reclaimed materials – cereal packets, tubes, cardboard packets. A pile of plastic tubs and containers. Plasticine or play dough, cotton wool and scraps of material, scissors, string, adhesive, sticky tape, drawing and colouring materials, pictures of chairs from magazines, white board and markers.

What to do
Remind the children that Baby bear's chair was broken and show them your small bear. Look at the pictures – naming parts of a chair and contrasting different types of seats. Look at the materials together. Demonstrate ways of cutting and fixing a cardboard tube to a flat cardboard surface, and show the children how to join plastic containers. Allow the children to experiment but ask them to practise first, so as not to waste materials. Decorate the finished chairs with materials, paper, felt-tipped pens or paint. Finally, display and discuss each model and invite the bear to relax in each seat!

Discussion
Name the parts of a chair and ask what they are for. Ask the children to describe their favourite chairs at home using the same terms, and note differences between chairs. What type of chair would the bear use at the table? Why? How is this different to the one he'd watch TV in?

For younger children
Model shapes of chairs using the play dough first. All make similar designs so that you can demonstrate joining techniques.

For older children
Allow a wider range of materials and greater experimentation, linking back more closely to the purpose of their design.

Follow-up activities
▲ Make model chairs or beds for the rest of the bear family.
▲ Ask the children to bring in photos of beds and chairs from home.
▲ Collect brochures and toy furniture for a furniture shop display.

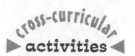

Breakfast build-ups

Objective
History – to focus on personal growth and development.

Group size
Four to eight children.

What you need
Pictures and photos of different breakfasts, including baby foods. Sample packets of baby, child and adult cereals, plus appropriate utensils and bowls, baby bottle and muslin, bibs and serviettes plus mats to distinguish the groupings. Long strip of card, pencils, paper, ruler and scissors. Table and chairs (highchair if possible). Low wall space and backing paper.

Preparation
Make up the baby cereals and leave to cool. Lay the table in age-related place settings, with a sample of each breakfast available. Cover wall space with backing paper.

What to do
Look at the place settings and ask the children to guess who they are for. Sit in the baby cereal place, put on the bib and ask the children to guess your age! If anyone has baby siblings, ask them to describe what they eat and how they feed. Show the pictures and discuss why tiny babies drink milk rather than eat.

Use this as an opportunity to consider how the children have grown and changed. Let them each have a go at sampling the different place settings, taking care with hygiene rules. Help the children to draw a simple card timeline. Decorate and mark with key ages before sticking on a wall. Now cut out the pictures of breakfast food and stick on the wall at the correct place on the line. Add helpful labels and comments as dictated by the children, and encourage them to draw pictures of things they could do

at each stage (guessing for the adult stage!) Use the timeline to highlight personal development, change and growth.

Discussion
Ask: can you feed yourself? Can you sit up on your own? Why do babies need a bib? Think carefully about how babies need to learn to do things like to sit up. Ask: what have you learned to do recently?

For younger children
Concentrate on baby/child comparisons. Help the children to develop a sense of pride in their personal achievements and progress.

For older children
Look in more detail at physical changes, and at what skills they have recently acquired or are learning now.

Follow-up activities
▲ Invite some real baby guests to breakfast, asking their parents about feeding habits and what their baby can/can't do yet.
▲ Place photos of family members along your timeline.
▲ Make a visual record of typical and healthy breakfasts for family members.

If you go down to the woods...

Objective

Geography – to extend awareness of different habitats.

Group size

Up to six children.

What you need

Pictures of real bears in natural habitats and in zoos (including polar bears), posters of woodland, desert, a busy town and Arctic scenery. Globe and selection of children's atlases. Paper and pencils, scissors, adhesive and collage materials – wood chips, sand, leaves and grasses, foil, material and paper. Books about bears.

What to do

Remind the children where the three bears lived and ask if real bears live in this way. Look together at the posters, describing each one and agreeing why bears might or might not choose to live there. Think about where bears might shelter and what they could eat.

Ask the children to choose one of these places for their bear to live. Start by drawing or painting a small bear, using this time to discuss details for their collage. Let the children select from the collage materials to create their habitat before sticking on their bear and adding details of his home and food.

Discussion

Ask the children about times they have seen wild animals, about the bear's appearance and what they think real bears eat. Ask: how could a real bear make a home and what food could he find? What do we mean by a wild animal? Why don't we have bears as pets? Encourage the children to learn the names of different types of scenery, such as mountains, forests and deserts, making simple comparisons between them.

For younger children

Help younger children to make their collages, keeping materials for different scenery separate.

For older children

Look at the maps and pictorial evidence which give clues as to where different types of bear live. Talk in more detail about how a bear's appearance gives clues about where they might live.

Follow-up activities

▲ Make a tape of the noises you might hear in each location and ask the children to guess which habitat you are in.
▲ Produce clues such as an ice-cube, sand, leaves, a brick and a rock, to match to different scenes.
▲ Act out an imaginary 'sensory' journey using songs such as 'If you go down to the woods today...'.

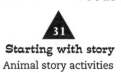

Who's been?...

Objective
Art – to develop skills of observational drawing.

Group size
Up to six children.

What you need
Thick paints in 'bear' colours, pencils, felt-tipped pens, paper, scissors, white board and markers, scrap paper.

Preparation
Paint three identical bear faces, paint another three, this time using a different shade of brown for one, making a cross face on another and giving a third an extra large nose. Cut enough paper for each child to make six bear faces.

What to do
Show the children your three identical bear faces and ask the children to describe what they look like. Now remove one of the identical faces and replace it with one of the different faces. Ask the children to tell you which is the odd-one-out. Can they tell you why? Repeat this activity a few times until the children are confident at describing the different faces.

Hand out three pieces of paper to the children and ask them to draw you three identical bear faces. Encourage careful copying to produce faces which are nearly the same. When they have done this, hand out the other three pieces of paper to each child and ask them to draw three faces that are different in some way. Suggest that they concentrate on changing just one feature to make the bears' faces different,

encouraging them to make the differences as slight as possible. Now ask the children to work with a partner to play games of odd-one-out and matching. Can they describe the different bears to each other accurately?

Discussion
Use mirrors and pictures to prompt discussion about facial features. Ask: how are eyes/mouths/noses different? What changes a face from looking happy to sad? What shapes and colours could we use for our bears?

For younger children
Let younger children use a template to draw their bear faces with. Suggest that they make very obvious changes for their 'odd-one-out bear', such as a colour change.

For older children
Look more closely at features and make the differences less obvious. Encourage the children to check for accuracy and try sticking on features using different media.

Follow-up activities
▲ Make a collage showing the bears in their cottage and include three mistakes to be found.
▲ Use mirrors and pastels to create your own 'portrait gallery'.
▲ Play 'guess who it is' describing games.
▲ Do all real bears look alike? Use reference material to promote observation.

Angry bear rap

Objective
Music – to understand that music can reflect moods.

Group size
Whole group introduction, follow-up with six children.

What you need
Cassette recorder, samples of music showing angry mood (such as 'Mars', *The Planets* (Holst) and relaxing mood (such as 'Albatross' by Fleetwood Mac). Pictures from magazines showing happy and cross faces. Selection of percussion instruments such as drums, bells, tamba, claves, wooden block and cymbals.

Preparation
Pre-record short samples of 'angry' and 'relaxing' music.

What to do
Listen carefully to the music samples, do they all inspire the same feelings? Show the different faces and ask the children to choose one to match each piece of music.

How did the bears feel as they came back to their house for breakfast, and how did their mood change? Model ways this could be reflected using one of the instruments to tap out a happy or relaxed rhythm, which becomes faster and angrier. After several examples using different instruments, ask for a volunteer to play, and for others to guess how the mood changes. Play a game using the picture faces, dealing one to a volunteer, who acts the 'mood' for others to guess. Experiment with different instruments, then make some recordings to be interpreted by other children.

Discussion
Ask: how do you behave when you are angry, what does it feel like and how do you control your temper? Describe colours and actions which match anger and then use these when playing the instruments. Think carefully about the quality of sound each instrument makes and about how this can be altered.

For younger children
Concentrate on developing listening skills, using strong contrasts for the children to describe fully. Experiment freely with two instruments before trying to mirror these different moods.

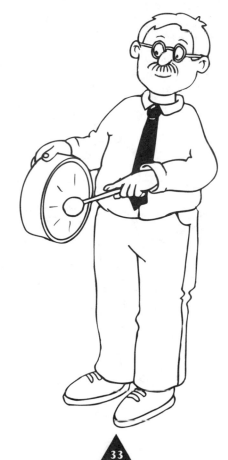

For older children
Ask the children to think of words they know which suggest anger, or to invent new words. Put their ideas together to create a rap-like accompaniment to your music.

Follow-up activities
▲ Make some simple recordings to act as a soundtrack for the original story.
▲ Make a dance to match your music.
▲ Draw and paint 'angry' patterns.
▲ Listen to different styles of music, finding 'angry' music from varying cultures.

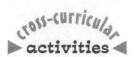

Big bear, little bear

Objective
PE – to explore big and little body movements and ways of travelling.

Group size
Whole group.

What you need
Samples of strong slow and heavy movement music, contrasted with quick and light music (taped).

What to do
Ask the children to find a space and to pretend to be one of the bears. I wonder which one? Ask them to show you who they are without making a sound and without bumping into other bears.

Listen to the different pieces of music and agree which bear each excerpt represents. Play the music and ask the children to move like the appropriate bear. Choose some children to demonstrate their movements to the others. Now make up a 'story' with the movements: sleeping in caves, stretching and searching for food. Ask the children to make these movements in a Big or Little bear fashion. Can the others guess which bear they are? Then ask the children to find a new way of moving around using a different part of their body, but still choosing to make either little or big movements.

Finally, play the music again and let the children respond creatively. Warm down by imagining the bears are preparing for bed and relaxing each part of their body before crawling off to sleep.

Discussion
Name big and little body parts. Ask: how can you move easily and quickly, and which parts can you only move slightly? Describe the contrasts as the children experiment. Ask: what are you using to balance on the floor and how are you moving along? Show me a different way. Describe how we can use our limbs in strong, purposeful ways and soft, flexible and varied movements.

For younger children
Focus on the quality of big and little movements.

For older children
Travel in contrasting ways, exploring different ways to balance and emphasise the quality of movements, both big and little.

Follow-up activities
▲ Use hoops and quoits to promote a wider range of movement and balance.
▲ Perform a 'Before and After' bear's dance, incorporating happy and angry movements.
▲ Make bear masks to aid bear dances.

34

Take care!

Objective
RE – to develop respect and caring for others and their possessions.

Group size
Any size is suitable.

What you need
Large sheets of paper, pens and pencils, pastels, scissors, adhesive sticks. Examples of popular play equipment. White board and markers.

What to do
Discuss how Goldilocks behaved in the story and what she might do if she came to visit us. Look at the examples of popular playthings and use Goldilocks to talk through regular problems with caring and sharing. Emphasise the co-operative behaviour you wish to promote through this activity.

On the white board, illustrate and label other areas of the room where care is required such as the home corner. Collect practical ideas to encourage being fair and discuss how to care for certain items, such as by cleaning and putting them away carefully. Make a note of things which can be altered and ask the children to help you remember by making their own 'Caring and Sharing' posters. This should be done in small groups so that they focus on working co-operatively.

Discussion
Ask the children to reflect upon times when they have not thought carefully about others. Ask: how do you look after your favourite toys? How would you feel if someone treated them badly? How can we remind others about sharing and caring for our things? Talk about the playthings in your group, checking that the children are aware of how to use and care for them.

For younger children
Concentrate on one activity or type of equipment, giving a step-by-step approach to playing and caring for them. Reinforce safety and social rules.

For older children
Help the children to decide which play areas to consider, showing them co-operative means of working. Encourage them to write helpful hints to put around the room.

Follow-up activities
▲ Make a list of ways to 'care and share' in the home corner.
▲ Make up 'I care for...' badges and posters to demonstrate how respect helps us get along together.
▲ Produce weekly tidying certificates for helpful children.

Starting with story
Animal story activities

Bears

glimpse of Goldilocks   glimpse of bears' cottage

Goldilocks and the three bears.

What a lovely day

Did you see something?

I'm hungry

tissue or crêpe paper

What you need

Large range of 'bear-coloured' scraps of material, fake fur, velvet, warm materials and wool. Bright thick yellow-gold wool. Crêpe and tissue paper, large buttons and beads, scissors, adhesive, backing paper and large grey paper, paints and colouring materials.

Preparation

Cover the boards with backing paper suitable for showing the bears out walking in the woods. Cut out paper into three bear sizes, some large scraps of paper for trees, part of Goldilocks and the cottage.

What to do

Talk to the children about what the bears did at the start of the story, and how they would feel setting off for their walk. Use the paints, crêpe and tissue paper to create a dense cover of trees and bushes in the background of your board. Make the upper part of Goldilocks using paper and golden wool, so that she can just be glimpsed dashing through the woods and add a section of the bear's cottage if you have

room. Next, depending on the size of your board, help the children to create a small, medium and large bear outline (or their upper bodies). Use the collage materials to match shades and textures to create three hairy bears. Use the buttons or crumpled tissue paper for bear features. Finally, create speech bubbles for the bears, filling them with suitable captions. Write out a label inviting the children to describe where Goldilocks is on the scene.

Discussion

Talk about suitable colours and textures for your collage, describing different shades with older children. Ask: what shall we use to make Goldilock's hair? How can we show that she is running? Invite the children to sort papers into three bear sizes.

Follow-up activities

▲ Make smaller 'lift the flap' pictures for finding Goldilocks or one of the objects described in the story.
▲ Make a display of bear-like textures and contrast them with cold, thin and hard materials.

Breakfasts

What you need

Collections of cereal packets, as varied as possible. Backing paper and two bright contrasting colours of sugar paper. Paper for designing packets, drawing/painting materials. Felt-tipped pens and lettering stencils. Breakfast utensils and a table or 'bar' display in front of wall space. Samples of cereal to taste-test (link to activity on page 28). Scissors, ruler, guillotine.

Preparation

Put up backing paper and cut up the sugar paper to make squares for a checked tablecloth. Let the children help you arrange it across the backing paper. Cut paper to match the sides of cereal packets and strips for labels.

What to do

Remind the children about the breakfast cereal tasting and encourage them to select two or three different empty packets. Help each child identify the name and key details of each product and talk about how the type of cereal is reflected in the name and artwork. Think about what makes each packet appealing. Ask the children to design and make up a name for their own cereal packets. Help them to put their ideas and

lettering onto the paper. Stencils and other equipment might be useful for older children. Leave to dry before sticking them on the sides of cereal boxes. Staple your designer boxes onto the tablecloth backing. (Add spoons, bowls and a milk jug/bottle to your table display.)

Now invite the children to come up with words to describe their invented cereals. Write these out and use them as display labels. Finally, let the children find a cloth and plastic utensils for the 'bar' in front of the wall display. Find bowls to match the bear sizes and have real 'variety' sized packets available for science activities.

Discussion

Ask the children to describe their chosen packets carefully, asking them where the name of their cereal is and where there are pictures. What do you think the cereal will taste like?

Follow-up activities

▲ Create a word bank and match the words to the appropriate cereals.
▲ Think of other food we eat at breakfast and make salt-dough rolls.
▲ Write out menus and build a breakfast bar in your role-play area.

Perfect porridge

Group size
Up to six children.

What you need
Measuring cup, wooden spoons, dessertspoons, teaspoons, knife, small bowls and tubs, shallow plastic dishes, grater, jug, two saucepans or two non-metallic bowls, hob. Aprons, washing and cleaning equipment. Magnifying glasses, photocopiable page 90 for each child, pencils. Ingredients: two types of varying porridge oats (not instant), soft brown sugar and caster sugar, small packet of raisins, salt, 50g cheese, grated chocolate, milk, water.

Preparation
Divide bowls and equipment to provide a 'tasting set' for each child. Photocopy the recording sheet on page 90.

What to do
Tell the children that you are going to cook porridge like the bears and remind the children about hygiene and safety rules. Compare the two types of porridge oats, looking at packets and using the magnifying glasses. Show the children the other ingredients, explaining that they're going to taste different flavours of porridge just like Goldilocks did.

Name each ingredient and look at them closely, predicting how they might change the porridge. Look at the grated chocolate and use the grater to demonstrate grating cheese. Allow each child to have a go. Cut the raisins into smaller pieces. Follow the packet instructions for making porridge (make enough for half a serving each). Use either the saucepan or the microwave method. Allow the children to measure with cups, to pour the liquid and oats, and to stir (away from the heat). Do the children notice how the appearance changes with cooking? Leave to cool slightly before putting small amounts in the bowls.

First, try the porridge on its own and demonstrate how the recording sheet works. Use the teaspoons to add or pour a tiny amount of each flavouring onto each bowl. Look at what happens, smell and then taste test each in turn. Help the children to record their results before clearing up and drawing conclusions.

Discussion
Encourage the children to use words and phrases such as: more and less liquid, thick and thin, lumpy and smooth. Use the sheet to prompt contrasts: is it sweet or savoury? Does it melt in or do you have to stir it? Compare big and small amounts of ingredients, why we use a tiny amount of some flavourings and what we used most of to make porridge.

Follow-up activities
▲ Make a Porridge Bar experimenting with new flavourings and offering instant too!

▲ Make flapjacks or a cheese flan with oats.

The Little Red Hen

This is a jolly tale brimming with different animal characters, starring a hard-working mother hen and her brood. There is a strong moral emphasis on the rewards of hard work but much of the humour comes from the shirking farmyard chorus. We also learn a great deal about the process of growing things and of making bread. You can opt for a traditional ending or a slightly kinder measure of justice to discuss with your children.

One morning Little Red Hen found some wheat seeds among her feed. 'Perfect for bread,' she said. 'Now who will help me plant these seeds?' She looked around hopefully at the other farmyard animals.

'Not I!' purred Cat, curling back to sleep.

'Not I!' barked Dog, snoozing in the sun.

'Not I!' grunted Pig, rolling over in the mud.

'Oh well,' sighed Hen, 'come on chicks let's do it ourselves'. So Hen tended and cared for those seeds. She hoed, weeded and watered them until the wheat was tall and strong, ready for harvesting. 'Who will help me harvest the wheat?' asked Hen hopefully.

'Not me!' yawned Cat, stretching out her claws.

'Not me!' barked Dog, chewing his bone.

'Not me!' grunted Pig, flipping her ears.

'Oh well,' sighed Hen, 'let's do it ourselves chicks'. So they did.

'Well now,' said Hen, 'who will help me take these sacks for milling?'

'Not I!' meowed Cat, turning the other way.

'Not I!' growled Dog, burying his bone.

'Not I!' grunted Pig, wallowing in her puddle.

So Little Red Hen heaved the heavy sacks onto a cart and tugged them down to the mill. She was tired when she got back, but she looked at her hungry chicks and said. 'Well now, who will help me make my bread?'

'Not Me!' hissed Cat, sneaking out of the kitchen.

'Not me!' barked Dog, sloping off for a snooze.

'Not me either!' grunted pig, waddling back to her sty.

'Oh well,' sighed Hen, putting on her apron. So Hen mixed and kneaded, she smoothed and shaped until four lovely loaves could be left to rise. She popped the bread in the oven and a delicious smell filled the room.

'Well now,' said Hen, 'who will help to eat my bread?' All the other animals rushed up.

'I will!' dribbled Dog, wagging his tail.

'I will!' purred Cat, eyes as big as saucers.

'I will!' grunted Pig, snorting and nosing.

'Oh No!' snapped Hen, with a shiver of feathers. 'You lazy lumps left the work up to me. So carry on watching... Here Chicks, fresh bread for tea!'

Starting with story
Animal story activities

Who will help me?

Objective
English – to develop vocabulary and to make up repetitive refrains.

Group size
Any size, with groups of up to four children when recording.

What you need
Cassette recorder, cleaning materials, washing up brush and bowl, cloth, shoes, dirty socks, construction bricks and other 'activity' prompts. White board and markers, copy of the story.

What to do
Re-tell the early stages of the story, asking for some volunteer Hens and animal characters in the question and answer choruses. Ask the children to think of times when they need help and record ways of asking for help on the board. Talk about the correct way to ask for help. Contrast asking and ordering, how do we feel about each way? Encourage role-play games using the props, such as the washing up bowl.

Now consider aspects of a daily getting-up routine when we might ask for help. Draw visual hints on the board to act as prompts and then encourage small groups of children to rehearse question and answer refrains, taking turns in each role. Then ask each group to make a recording, choosing a variety of co-operative and unhelpful responses to a series of four or five questions. Play them back and discuss with the other children.

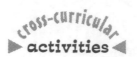

Discussion
Focus on words we use to ask for help, listening to how tones and patterns change between a question and a response. Ask: how would you get help with making your breakfast? What would you say and who would you ask? Talk about different responses to different types and tones of voice, and of how we can 'answer' without speaking. Decide which are kind and unkind ways of responding.

For younger children
Use role-play to build confidence in speaking and responding in clear, deliberate sentences and offer close support when recording.

For older children
As confidence grows, encourage a wider use of language, more elaborate responses and greater characterisation. Encourage the social skills involved in successful shared recordings.

Follow-up activities
▲ Make individual or large zigzag books with a drawing and speech bubble request and flaps below to lift showing alternative answers.
▲ Complete photocopiable page 91 to develop fine motor skills. Use it as an opportunity to talk about the lazy creatures and how they could have helped.

Guess what I do?

Objective
English – to explore non-verbal ways of communicating and to use action words.

Group size
Any size is suitable.

What you need
Coloured paper or card for making a large book, plain paper, drawing and writing materials, scissors and adhesive sticks.

Preparation
Cut card or paper so that each child can have a page in a large book. Trim plain paper, labelling and writing paper so that it fits neatly.

What to do
Discuss what activities the Hen performed in the story. Mime some of these actions for the children to guess, before encouraging volunteers to do the same. Try singing the Hen's actions (to the tune of 'Here we go round the Mulberry Bush'). For example: 'This is the way we knead the dough...'

Now encourage each child to mime something they've been doing earlier in the day for others to guess. You can now use the children's mime poses to make careful drawings about the things they love doing. Collect ideas, but encourage individual responses so that each child makes a personal contribution with a written or dictated caption. Share and discuss together, then stick in each contribution to make an action-packed 'doing book'.

Discussion
Focus the children's attention on the actions by asking: what's she doing with her hands/feet/eyes/and so on? How can you tell he likes doing that? What do you think she is holding? Ask the children why their chosen activity is special.

For younger children
Offer simple mimes for the children to interpret and copy. Describe each activity sequence carefully and fully.

For older children
Encourage creative and individual responses allowing the children scope to practise their own miming and descriptive skills. Let the children plan and present their page as independently as possible.

Follow-up activities
▲ Make a collection of activities they don't like doing and write down why.
▲ Find out what most children like doing in their spare time and ask them to make posters.
▲ Show a visual sequence of actions with one stage missing and ask the children to spot what's wrong (such as forgetting to pour milk on your cereal).

building lego

hugging my teddy

me painting

reading my book.

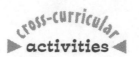

Measuring shoots

Objective
Mathematics – to develop skills of non-standard measure.

Group size
Up to six children.

What you need
Plasticine, boards, tomato plants (or similar), play dough, string, mathematical cubes, rulers, tape-measures, paper and pencils.

Preparation
Make 'shoots' of different lengths using Plasticine and green rope or string. Ensure that the visual difference is appropriate for your children. Bring in samples of differently sized shoots, such as tomato plants.

What to do
Remind the children that the Hen grew wheat from seeds. Look at your plants and discuss whether they are exactly or nearly the same size. Challenge the children to find out which shoot is the biggest and which of your Plasticine shoots is the smallest. Now curl the longest one around and ask the same question, curling it out again to show how it's still the same height.

Ask the children to make three differently sized shoots with play dough and then give them to a friend to put in order of size. (Be aware of any difficulties that may arise, such as those very similar or of varying widths.) Finish by asking the children to draw around their tallest finger on the paper. Then ask them to draw a shoot which is smaller than their finger and one that is larger than their finger. Label them clearly.

Discussion
When comparing heights ask the children whether the shoots start from the same position. Ask: which is the smallest? How can you tell which is the tallest? What happens when a shoot is bendy? Can you think of ways to measure it?

For younger children
Start by comparing just two shoots, ensuring that the concepts and language are secure. Allow experimentation with cubes and measures but don't go beyond visual guessing.

For older children
Use the finger exercise to demonstrate the need for standard measure, by using your own middle finger or the child's small finger. Give the children plenty of experience of using cubes and string to make non-standard measurements.

Follow-up activities
▲ Keep a weekly record of the growth rate of your plants.
▲ Find objects around the room which are 'smaller/larger or nearly the same height as' one of your shoots.
▲ Draw three shoots on large squared paper and count 'how many squares high' they are.

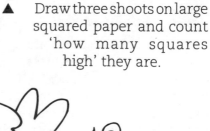

Lazy pets, lively pets

Objective
Mathematics – to develop a range of recording methods.

Group size
Up to six children.

What you need
Six clipboards, six small pictures of typical pet animals (of similar size), coloured pencils, pencils, large squared paper and columns of squared paper (enough for two pieces each), scissors, adhesive sticks.

What to do
Talk about which animals in the story were lazy and ask whether anyone has a lazy pet or a lively pet at home. Show the children the six animal pictures and ask them to identify and describe them. Make sure the children understand lazy and lively behaviour.

Give each child a clipboard, one of the animal pictures and two columns of graph paper. Agree together one colour for lazy and another for lively. Ask the children to conduct a survey by asking the children in their group: do you think this animal is lazy or lively? Fill in one square in the correct colour and column to represent each answer. Each researcher will finish up with two coloured columns that can be easily compared. Show the children how to make a simple graph with their results. Place the labelled photos evenly along the horizontal axis. Mark off numbers along the vertical axis to match the square count on the coloured columns. Help the children trim and stick on the columns so that the results may be clearly read.

Discussion
Show the children how to count the number of children interviewed ensuring that this tallies with the number of responses. Give the children practice in interpreting the graph by asking questions such as: how many children said (cats) are lazy? How many thought they were lively? How many altogether?

For younger children
Limit the number of people to be interviewed and use mathematical cubes of two different colours (from boxes with either a lively or a lazy face on the side) instead of paper.

For older children
Help the children to devise a simple recording process and make simple comparisons with the results. Focus on what makes the graph easy to 'read'.

Follow-up activities
▲ Look at other simple recording methods, putting a cube in the appropriate hoop, then comparing the tallies.
▲ Make a pictogram of the children's real pets to find out which animal is most popular.
▲ Find out about animals who are particularly sleepy or active.

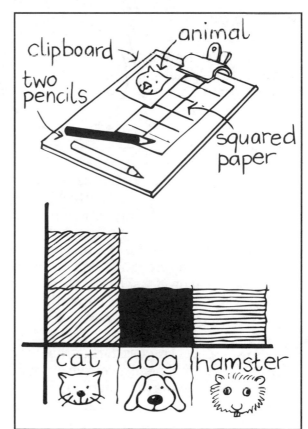

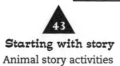

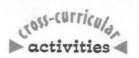

Need it to grow?

Objective

Science – to compare living/non-living things and to understand conditions for growth.

Group size

Up to six children.

What you need

Fast growing seeds such as mung beans, mustard and cress, small pots and compost (peat-free), clear containers, toy watering can, set of gardening tools and pieces of card. Objects to sort such as a doll, a stone, a feather, a plant and a worm. Two sorting circles, paper and drawing materials.

Preparation

Use card to write out labels: 'Living/not living' and 'Can grow/can't grow', each with a picture clue. Attach one of the labels to each of the sorting circles.

What to do

Remind the children what Hen had to do to help the seeds grow. Talk about the things around us and discuss which things grow and are living. Look carefully at the selection of objects and use the labelled sorting circles to divide them into living/non-living and then repeat by dividing them into can grow/can't grow. Let the children sort the items alone and explain their reasons for selection. Now look at the seeds carefully and discuss where and how they should be planted. Discuss the fact that they will need a certain amount of water and light, and then plant them carefully. Make a weekly check on your crop.

Discussion

Ask the children how they know if something is alive. Encourage the children to consider factors such as: does it move/breathe/change/grow? Look at the seeds together and discuss why they haven't changed. Ask: what do they need to help them grow? Consider factors such as light, water and soil. Ask: what happens to plants without any light? What happens if they have too much or too little water? Can plants grow without any soil? (Some will root well in water alone.)

For younger children

Make clear contrasts between living and non-living and show them some simple ways of caring for plants.

For older children

Think in more detail about the character-istics of living and non-living and of growing and non-growing. Investigate whether a plant needs soil and/or light to grow, and how much water it needs.

Follow-up activities

▲ Design a seed packet cover, drawing ways they should be planted and cared for.
▲ Grow beans in clear plastic containers so that their root system can be seen.
▲ Make a contrasting collage to show what plants need to grow successfully and what *we* need to grow.

Watering machine

Objective
Design and Technology – to create a 'watering machine' and learn about water flow.

Group size
Four to six children.

What you need
Plenty of space, water tray, cloths and mops, plastic tubing and pipes, reclaimed plastic containers and bottles (some with holes in and with different lips), watering can with sprinkling cap that can be removed, ladle, plastic masking tape, sieves, straws, small buckets, plastic mesh. Knitting needle and heat source. Pictures of different forms of irrigation (try old Oxfam calendars), hose and spray catalogues. Plants in a small trough of soil, another trough and a small amount of (peat-free) compost.

Preparation
Make holes of different sizes and numbers in plastic with a heated knitting needle (make sure the children are standing well back). Set some clear rules about keeping water in the tray to avoid accidents.

What to do
Remind the children how Hen watered her plants and invite them to make a machine to help her. Look at the pictures of hoses, sprays, ditches, wells and so on. Show the plants in a trough and ask someone to use the can to water them carefully. Notice how the flow is gradual. Show the children the difference in flow when the sprinkling cap of the watering can is removed.

Now allow the children to use the materials to experiment with flow, to make something which sprinkles gently and something which pours fast. Encourage them to think about ways that water can be moved from one place to the next, experimenting with carrying, channelling and funnelling and how the tubing and hoses might be joined to transport the water from one end of the trough to the other.

Finally, fill the spare trough with some soil and place at the end of the water tray. Encourage the children to produce a slow flow of water to 'rain' gently on the soil.

Discussion
Ask: how can you stop and start the flow of water? Think about beach and sand play to remind the children of channels and consider what we use to carry water in. Experiment with pouring and with the size and number of holes poured through.

For younger children
Limit the exercise to pouring and learning how to influence the flow of the water.

For older children
Allow some time to experiment and encourage the children to work co-operatively.

Follow-up activities
▲ Explore dams and irrigation systems using sand and water.
▲ Draw a poster showing where water is used at home and how it is moved around.

Flower tray

Harvesting history

Objective
History – to learn about the changes in the ways crops are harvested.

Group size
Four to eight children.

What you need
Pictures and photos of horse-drawn ploughs, oxen, sickles, tractors and combine harvesters. Drawing materials, chalk, crayons and pastels, paper. Samples of wheat and barley, plus other familiar crops. Photocopiable page 92.

Preparation
Try to visit an arable farm and invite a retired farm-worker to describe how things have changed.

What to do
Look at the pictures of farming machinery and guess what they are used for. Hen cared for her seeds by hand alone, why don't farmers do this? Think about three stages of growing crops, using photocopiable page 92 as a talking point.

Ask one set of children to draw how Hen would have done each task, another group to use the photocopiable sheet and books to draw how this might have been done long ago, and a third group to draw modern methods. Help the children in their research and label each picture clearly so that it can be shown as a comparative display.

Discussion
Ask how Hen planted the seeds and what she did to care for them. Discuss times the children have helped in the garden, why weeding is necessary and how to do it. What do they use to dig and weed? What do they use to water plants and how can they tell when food is ready for picking (harvesting)? Look at farming tools and machinery and ask: how do these help the farmer?

For younger children
Help younger children to appreciate how machines help us, by comparing doing things by machines and by hand. Help the children to keep their drawings simple.

For older children
Look more closely at the materials and design of old machines and notice advances in technology and the types of skills required by a farmer.

Follow-up activities
▲ Cut a small section of grass with scissors, compare this with the speed of mowing.
▲ Try scattering seeds evenly by hand and spend time weeding the garden.
▲ Find out how harvest time is celebrated around the world, and about traditional activities in your own area.
▲ Use photocopiable page 92 to sort the pictures into now and then and to practise ordering sequentially.

Bread basket

Objective
Geography – to appreciate that a crop grows better in some places than others.

Group size
Up to six children.

What you need
Bread wrappers, toy tractors, stones, soil, sand, leaves and construction blocks. Six old baking tray tins, crushed ice-cubes, soil and grass, green play dough. Pictures of arable fields, rocky mountains, a crowded city, a jungle and a desert. Clean lolly stick and sticky paper.

Preparation
Remind the children that Hen had to grow wheat to make her bread. Look at some bread wrappings. Examine the picture scenes carefully and describe each landscape.

What to do
Tell the children that you are going to model different types of land so they can compare how it feels to drive their tractor over each one. Divide out the materials and equipment and help them use the sand to make a strip of 'desert', followed by 'mountain' rocks, a green play dough 'jungle' and a soil/grass 'field'. Help the children to make some simple comparisons – it's hard to find space for your tractor in building block city, but there's plenty of room in the sandy desert. Make a simple banner using the lolly stick and sticky paper for the children to stick into the ground which they think best for farming.

Discussion
Ask the children what the surface of each location looks and feels like, what is the same and what is different. Discuss how the land is used, what's growing on it, what's been built on it and so on. Describe how easy or hard it is to drive your tractor over this land, and how the weather helps or hinders growth.

For younger children
Enjoy making each surface together, focusing on the main differences in appearance and texture.

For older children
Look at other influences such as the weather, roads and where people live.

Follow-up activities
▲ Make a collage of different scenes and annotate with reasons why they might not be chosen by your farmer. Show the farmer in her perfect spot.
▲ Hold a toy tractor ploughing competition over different surfaces.
▲ Look at atlases and maps to locate some of the farming areas. Match this to the origins shown on cereals, flour and so on.

▲ 47
Starting with story
Animal story activities

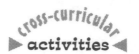
Red hen hands

Objective

Art – to make a hand-print collage and to focus on shades of colour and cutting skills.

Group size

Up to six children.

What you need

Thick paints in shades of red, brown, orange and yellow, mixing palettes, brushes, paper, scissors, sticky paper, straw, sponge, blue and green paint, and pieces of card, backing paper.

Preparation

Prepare the backing paper, space for your prints to dry and for children to print onto the background. Cut pieces of paper into rough 'hand' sizes.

What to do

Explain that you're going to make a giant picture of Hen among her corn, and that her feathers will be made from hand prints. Name and describe the range of colours and demonstrate how mixing light and dark will generate a new colour. Ask the children to select two different colours and to make three hand prints, one with each separate colour and then one when they are mixed together.

Leave the prints to dry while they clear up. Work on sponge printing the sky and use the side of card to print green blades of grass. Arrange the straw in among the grass.

Return to your hands and help each child to cut around their prints, showing them how to turn the paper and to leave a gap around any narrow bits. Overlap the prints to create a giant fluffy hen and use sticky paper to add the features – beak, eye and claws.

Discussion

Ask the children about their favourite colours, and name those you are going to use. Can they show you the lightest and the darkest? Are any of the colours nearly the same? Look closely at what happens when two colours are mixed and describe the changes.

For younger children

Experiment with three colours only and supervise cutting closely to avoid disappointment.

For older children

Encourage experimentation and mixing. Aim for accurate prints and less supervised cutting, with the children choosing how to paint and print background scenery.

Follow-up activities

▲ Ask the children to dictate what Hen is saying and add collage chicks and lazy animals.
▲ Paint other pictures using only 'Hen' colours.
▲ Use a relaxing colour like blue, to focus on mixing different shades and using the results to create fantastic patterns.

Musical requests

Objective
Music – to appreciate the voice as an instrument and to make question/answer refrains.

Group size
Any size is suitable.

What you need
Animal cards to match the farmyard creatures used in your story, simple pitched instrument such as a recorder.

Preparation
Use magazine photos or draw your own simple animal card picture clues.

What to do
Explain to the children that they're going to help put Hen's questions and the animal's replies to music. Say the phrases together and notice how voices naturally go up and down as we speak. Use the recorder to demonstrate high and low notes and then make these contrasts with your voice.

Ask the first part of Hen's question, 'Who will help me...?' and point out that we can say words at different speeds too. Put your question to a simple tune as you tap out the beat with your fingers. Repeat in the same way with your animal replies, encouraging the children to join in with you. Once the children are more confident, talk about the various animals' characteristics so that their 'reply' varies in pitch, tone and

tempo. Use the cards to deal out these personalities and ask the remaining children to take turns at being Hen, encouraging all to have a go.

Discussion
Use words like beat, rhythm and speed to focus on tempo, encouraging strong contrasts. Ask: how would the cat sing? Would the pig sing in the same way? Show me how.

For younger children
Concentrate on good listening skills and on appreciating the variety of sounds produced, rather than on accuracy.

For older children
Celebrate voice power and allow the children to create freely to increase their confidence and understanding. Ask them to count and tap out beats and to describe the changes in pitch accurately. Keep this simple, short and successful.

Follow-up activities
▲ Make recordings of your animal parade!
▲ Move in response to your tunes and rhythm.
    ▲ Use favourite songs and 'fit' the words to them.

Busy hen or lazy lumps?

Objective
PE – to contrast effort of movement with relaxation and keeping still.

Group size
Whole group.

What you need
Tambourine, hoops. Props such as a pillow, blanket, book, sun-glasses, radio, rope, trainers, racket and soft-ball, dancing shoes.

What to do
Ask the children to find a space, moving as slowly and heavily as possible. Once in their space, go loose and floppy, before curling on the floor. Now jiggle each body part awake, starting with rapid toe and finger movements. Stretch out and feel your body getting powerful and strong. To the beat of the tambourine, ask the children to dart quickly around the room like Hen. When you hit the tambourine hard, ask them to relax completely. Repeat the game, looking for children who are moving in interesting ways.

Now place the hoops around the room, putting an 'energetic' or 'relaxing' prop in some of them. Discuss each of the props and ideas for movement that symbolise them. For example dancing and twirling movements would represent the hoop containing dancing shoes. Ask the children to make fast, energetic movements or slow, lazy ones in response to the tambourine. On hearing a loud beat, the children make a small group around their nearest hoop and decide how to act out the activity together.

Finish by moving in a slow, deliberate way back to get changed.

Discussion
Ask the children if they know what skills and parts of their body they are using. Talk about regular hobbies and pastimes, deciding whether they are mainly exercise or relaxation, letting the children appreciate that both are valuable.

For younger children
Help younger children to understand the different types of beat and how they should respond to them. They will need help to work co-operatively.

For older children
Encourage them to develop unusual ways of responding to the tambourine.

Follow-up activities
▲ Make masks for Hen and the other creatures.
▲ Make a collection of photos showing how families relax and take exercise.
▲ Produce a pictogram showing favourite playtime activities.

Many fingers make...

Objective
RE – to understand the reasons for sharing and co-operating.

Group size
Groups of three to four children.

What you need
Timers, construction set, play dough, four pots of paint and four brushes, large sheet of scrap paper. Sand tray, large wide container and four teaspoons. Farm set (such as those from Early Learning Centres).

Preparation
Arrange the materials around the room so that groups can move between different tasks. Possible tasks could be filling the container with sand using only teaspoons, building a farm and putting toy animals in each field, making a construction city, making a dough sausage as long as the table and so on.

What to do
Discuss times that the children work alone, and times they work together. Hen didn't want to work alone, and yet only her baby chicks would help her. Explain that you're going to test out working alone and together, to find out about sharing and co-operating. Show the children the timers and describe one of the tasks, such as covering the sheet of paper with paint so there are no gaps. Ask for a Hen volunteer and watch her struggle with the task for one minute. Then call for volunteer animals to don their aprons and join in. Let the other children notice how much more has been achieved (make sure you focus on doing things together rather than competitively).

Model each of the activities with a different set of children so they all practise

doing and watching. Ask how each 'Hen' felt working alone and then as part of a team. Talk about being fair when clearing up and how much easier it is when everyone helps.

Discussion
Talk about tasks they prefer to do alone and about a time when they had fun sharing. Think about a difficult play area. Ask: what are the problems with working together? How do you decide about taking turns? Who decides what to do and how can you settle arguments? Discuss how you feel when you are left out or when the tidying isn't shared.

For younger children
Talk about the times when someone has helped them to do something that they found difficult to do on their own.

For older children
Give the children more scope to make mistakes and to describe their feelings when encountering difficulties. Agree simple rules and offer support to ensure teamwork is successful.

Follow-up activities
▲ Make a hand print display and examples of when 'Many fingers make light work.'
▲ Make up 'Helping Hands Awards' – badges and posters for children who have been particularly helpful.
▲ Make a book showing how the children help at home.

Flour power

children's drawings of wheat

white flour trail

3D flour packet

What you need
Sample flour packet, a few spoonfuls of flour. Pictures of food which contain flour, paper, newspaper, paints, drawing materials. Heads of wheat, sketching paper and pencils, magnifying glasses. Scissors, adhesive. Backing paper and contrasting sugar paper for mounting sketches. Protective floor covering.

Preparation
Put up plain backing paper using a colour which will highlight white flour trails and line-drawing sketches. Put floor covering under the display wall.

What to do
Ask the children what crop Hen grew and how it had to be changed before she could cook with it. Show the children the heads of wheat and use magnifying glasses to prompt careful sketches using the special pencils and paper. Mount work and then use to create a decorative border around your display board. Fill your empty flour packet with newspaper and attach it to the centre of your display. Using adhesive and shakes of flour, catching the dustings on the floor covering, help the children make five small

trails of flour fanning out from the packet. While this is drying, look through the food pictures to prompt ideas about how we use flour in cooking. Help the children paint or draw a wide range of these. When dry, sort into five groups such as cakes, biscuits, pastry, bread and soups, gravy and so on.

Ensure that there are at least three items the same and that there are five current buns to spot. Staple these sets at the end of each flour trail. Label and let the children devise key items for people to spot.

Discussion
As the children look at the wheat develop their observational skills by asking: what shapes can you see? Is it the same colour/thickness/feel all the way down? As they are drawing their food, remind them to make it as 'tasty' as possible by thinking about shape, size, colour and decoration.

Follow-up activities
▲ Find out about how wheat is harvested and make a simple sequence chart.
▲ Make a sequence chart of how Hen grew and cared for her wheat crop.
▲ Collect samples of corn, wheat, oats and barley, and try printing with them.

Helping hands

children's cut out hands with drawings concealed underneath

children's illustrations

Helping hands

stick on numbers to show the order of Little Red Hen's jobs

cut out numbers with Velcro back

we use these things with our hands

hand cream

gloves

puppets

hand puppet

guess whats inside

feely bag

What you need

Shades of red, orange, yellow and brown paints, pastels and drawing materials, gloves, hand puppets, writing implements, small pieces of sugar paper, backing paper, white board and markers, Velcro. Table display, feely bag containing small objects – brush, duster, pencil, rolling pin, ball and so on. Scissors, adhesive. Pen and labelling card.

Preparation

Put up backing paper which will contrast with the red hand prints.

What you do

Talk to the children about the jobs that Hen had to do, and sequence them together by drawing objects on the board. Remind the children of the Red hen hands (page 48) activity and ask about times when they have been helpful.

Hold up your hands and think about how essential they are for eating, cleaning, washing, dressing, drawing and so on. Now ask the children to make bold red hand prints on the sugar paper, using the colours to explore different shades. While these are drying, use drawing materials for each child to record one example of how they are helpful. (Small enough to be concealed under the hand prints.)

Look at your pictorial list of Little Red Hen's jobs and ask pairs of children to draw an illustration for each one using pastels. Mount these and arrange them randomly along the bottom of your display board. Make Velcro tags with numbers on and write out a label inviting the children to stick on numbers to show the correct order.

Cut out and secure the hands to the board so that they can be opened to reveal the children's examples of how they are helpful. Finally, use the table space for your display of objects related to hands, plus a feely bag containing items illustrating 'handy jobs' such as a brush and a rolling pin.

Discussion

Think carefully about how we use our hands for different jobs. Ask the children to mime doing 'helpful tasks' and ask: what are you doing? How are you helping? Encourage the children to retell the story, ordering each of Hen's tasks so they are able to retell what she did first, second...last.

Follow-up activities

▲ Explore other uses for hands – clapping, catching, measuring.
▲ Think about how we care for and clean our hands.

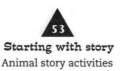

Bread buns

Group size
Up to six children.

What you need
Weighing scales, small bowls and large mixing bowl, tablespoons, teaspoons, jug, wooden spoon, plastic food wrap, kitchen roll, knife, fork, palette knife, sieve, baking trays, pastry brush, wire rack. Aprons, oven, oven gloves and cleaning equipment. Margarine/butter wrappers for greasing. Ingredients: 500g strong white flour, half pint warm water, two level teaspoons dried yeast, two level teaspoons sugar, one level teaspoon salt, a little milk. (Makes 16.)

What to do
Explain to the children that they are going to make bread, just like Hen did. Talk about why the yeast is important before adding the sugar and four tablespoons of warm water to it. Let them all help stir and then leave the mixture in a warm place. Observe every five minutes or so, until its frothy (after about 20 minutes). Use this time to examine the other ingredients as you weigh each out carefully. Let each child have a go at sieving the flour and salt into a large mixing bowl and make a well in the middle. Add the frothy yeast and the rest of the water gradually, mixing with a wooden spoon. Continue until it forms a dough and give each child a lump to knead on a floured surface for about 10 minutes. (Show them how to do this.)

Wrap the bread and leave it to rise for at least an hour. (Wash up then return to other activities, so the children can appreciate the delay involved.) Heat the oven to 220°C (425°F, Gas Mark 7). Grease the baking trays and discover what's happened to the dough mix. Cut the dough into roll-sized pieces and divide evenly among the children. Let them experiment with making bun shapes, showing them how to make a sausage and twist it up. Put the finished buns on baking trays and leave to rise again in a warm place while you clear up. Brush each with a little milk then pop in the oven for about 15 minutes. Tap them underneath to hear if they're cooked (they should sound hollow).

Discussion
Discuss what yeast looks and smells like and describe the strange frothing. Talk about wet and dry ingredients, about how the water mix changes the flour. What does the dough feel like, how does it stretch and respond to prods? What parts of your hands are used in kneading, why do you think we need to do it for so long? Talk about the different techniques used in kneading – stretch, push, fold over, out and in and so on.

Follow-up activities
▲ Add dried fruit or cheese to your bread. Decorate the tops.
▲ Use different flours and find new bread recipes from different cultures.
▲ Taste some unusual breads.

The Three Billy Goats Gruff

This tale celebrates teamwork and determination. It is full of challenge and drama, showing the need to confront our fears head on. Although it raises many difficult issues, children take comfort in the fact that it is the little goat who takes the lead and so enjoys her reward first. The characters in this tale may be stern and frightening, but it may be told in a number of ways and offers safe ways of discussing fears and negative emotions.

Once there was a herd of goats who lived on one side of a steep gorge. On the other side they could see lush green grass, but where they lived the ground was rocky and bare. Now, to reach the grass there was an old wooden bridge across the river, but this was guarded by a terrible troll.

One day, three hungry goats, one big, one medium and one tiny, decided enough was enough and they trotted down to the bridge. With a skip and a jump, tiny Billy Goat Gruff trotted up to the bridge. Her fast little hooves echoed trip-trap, trip-trap as she trotted over the wooden planks. Just as she got to the middle, up jumped the terrible troll, 'Who dares cross my bridge?' he bellowed. 'I'm going to eat you all up from your horns to your hooves!'

'Oh no, don't eat me, I'm much too small,' pleaded tiny Billy Goat Gruff. 'Why not wait for my sister, she's much juicier.'

Troll had to admit the goat was only a bite-size, so he growled, 'Very well, be off with you before I change my mind'.

Tiny Billy Goat Gruff bolted over the bridge and sunk into the soft grass meadow.

When the medium Billy Goat Gruff saw her kid sister tucking into that sweet grass, she knew she must follow. So trip-trap, trip-trap went her hooves on the planks as she tottered over the bridge. Suddenly the terrible troll leaped up in front of her, so big he blotted out the sun. 'Who dares cross my bridge?' he bellowed. 'I'm going to eat you all up from your horns to your hooves.'

'Oh wait, don't eat me!' pleaded medium Billy Goat Gruff. 'If you wait a minute longer, my brother will come this way. He's twice the size of me.' As the troll was very hungry, he burbled, 'Be off with you, before I change my mind'. She took a flying leap and landed next to her sister in the meadow.

That just left big Billy Goat Gruff, who was very big and brave. When his hooves touched the bridge they made a huge clashing trip-trap like thunder and the terrible troll leaped up to block his path. 'Who's this who dares to cross my bridge. I'm going to eat you!' he yelled.

The big Billy Goat Gruff lowered his head, 'Oh no you're not Troll,' he thundered. With a snort and a toss of his mighty horns, he lifted that terrible troll so high in the air he flew through the clouds and was never seen again. The big Billy Goat Gruff joined his sisters in the meadow where they lived happily for the rest of their lives.

In, on and under

Objective
English – to develop use of positional language.

Group size
Up to six children.

What you need
Toy trolls – one between two children. Boxes, white paper. Photocopiable page 93, card, scissors and pencils. Pieces of brown paper. Thick green, brown, blue, yellow, purple and red paints.

Preparation
Make three sizes of goat templates out of card using the photocopiable sheet, cut up matching sizes of brown paper. Hide three trolls around the room.

What to do
Retell the start of the story, discussing where the goats wanted to go and how they had to get there. Suggest you play a game hiding trolls in different places. Use a box and bricks to demonstrate a range of positional terms, asking the children: is the troll on/in/behind the box? Let the children take turns doing the same until they are confident with the terms used.

Now encourage the children to ask questions to locate the trolls that you have hidden around the room. Introduce terms such as 'near' and 'opposite' by giving clues until the trolls are found.

Make a fingerprint paint scene using the thick paints. Using the card goat templates and brown paper, invite the children to cut out their three goats and stick them on to their painted scene. Show them how to paint a troll using purple and red fingerprints.

Discussion
Start with familiar words, asking the children to put their troll 'in, on, under and next to' a box. Note any difficulties and repeat the exercise in different ways. Ask the children to tell you where an ojbect is, or hide something for you to find. Relate the position of different objects – the goat is between the bridge and the tree and so on.

For younger children
Limit the range of language used, so that they use it with understanding and confidence. Concentrate on practical 'putting and looking' activities rather than making and describing.

For older children
Introduce and use new terms to the children as their confidence grows. Encourage co-operative pair work and greater accuracy in their recording.

Follow-up activities
▲ Make a picture map to show the journey which the goat made.
▲ Use positional terms and your goat maps in PE sessions.
▲ Let the children play hide and seek games with their trolls and the construction material.
▲ Let volunteers draw a troll on the board adding a bridge, tree and so on, and then using positional language to describe where the troll is.

Who's that trip-trapping?

Objective
English – to write simple descriptions to create a guessing game book.

Group size
Up to six children.

What you need
White board and markers, paper, drawing and writing materials, goat templates (photocopiable page 93). Samples of 'goat's fur', horns and 'beard' material. Beads (for eyes).

Preparation
Cut and fold paper to make a simple four-page zigzag book for each child.

What to do
Discuss what question the troll asked each time he heard someone on the bridge. Let the children act out this part of the story, focusing on the differences between each goat. Ask the children to imagine that the troll can't hear the hooves, so think of visual and character clues to describe each goat, drawing the children's ideas on the board. Use fur and other props to help the children remember the key features of the goats. Make up some simple size and character related clues, such as: 'I've got shiny tiny hooves and I love prancing...'; 'I've got black beady eyes as big as saucers...' and so on. Use the clues to play a guessing game.

Show the children the book design and explain that you want them to think up three to four clues for one of the goats. Use the template or draw a picture of the goat on the other side (not on the cover). Illustrated clues can then be read before turning the book to reveal the goat's identity.

Discussion
Explore language linked to size – small/tiny/little/minute and so on. Let the children enjoy learning and using a new word. Look at the 'props' and ask: what is it's shape? What does it feel like? What would the big goat's horns be like? What sort of voice does your goat have and how does it move?

For younger children
Write out simple clues together but avoid giving away the name of the goat! Simplify the book to create two to three shared clues and stick to strong comparisons between the big and tiny goat characters.

For older children
Encourage more original clues and greater detail in the pictures. Help the children copy or write some of the text independently. Work co-operatively to test out how effective their clues are.

Follow-up activities
▲ Make a multi-textured goat collage, so that each has a distinctive feel.
▲ Make up a sound track of goat family clues.
▲ Create guessing books based on family and friends.

▲ **57**
Starting with story
Animal story activities

Bridge patterns

Objective
Mathematics – to practise following a simple sequence and pattern.

Group size
Up to six children.

What you need
String or thread for each child, a variety of beads of different colours and shapes. Paper, pencils and felt-tipped pens to match the bead colours.

Preparation
Ensure there are sufficient duplicates for copying bead patterns.

What to do
Ask the children to work with a partner, each having a thread with a knotted end and sharing a small selection of beads. Show them how to make a bead 'bridge' starting with only four to five beads. Ask them to describe the beads you have used, 'reading' from left to right. Make different patterns with beads using colour or shape as variables, asking the children to describe your bridge each time.

Now ask the children to work with a partner to make patterns for each other to copy and describe. Extend the number of beads or the complexity of the pattern when children are confident. Ask them to continue each other's patterns, showing them how to 'detect' the pattern and repeat it. When the children have chosen their favourite pattern ask them to copy it accurately onto a piece of paper. Ask others to 'guess' their pattern from this visual guide.

Discussion
Ask the children to sort and match the beads, describing their properties. Ask: can you find me another cube/a blue sphere? and so on, until they are able to find without copying. Ask: what shapes are the sides? Has it got corners? Include positional and ordinal terms: what bead comes first/next/second/last?

For younger children
Limit the range of beads and the length of string and concentrate on one attribute at a time until the children understand the process and concepts involved.

For older children
Let the children experiment and set each other more complex patterns involving counting beads and contrasting other attributes.

Follow-up activities
▲ Use regular 2D shapes to make sticky paper bridges.
▲ Find out about the names and properties of the 3D bead shapes you encounter.
▲ Build bridges with a variety of construction equipment and discuss the shapes used.
▲ Make some accurate plans and diagrams of your room.

Forward and back

Objective
Mathematics – to reinforce number sequence and value.

Group size
Up to six children.

What you need
Flooring suitable for chalking on, coloured chalk, small pebbles, card, thick pens, pencils and drawing materials. Dice.

Preparation
Make large cards for the symbols 0–6.

What to do
Discuss with the children how the goats had to make their way step by step over the troll's bridge.

Set up an imaginary bridge, by marking the beginning and end of the bridge with chairs and chalking the rest of the bridge shape on to the floor. Now count the number of strides that are needed to go over the bridge (managing the span so that it produces six steps). Repeat again and then let the children count their way across.

Use the chalks to create coloured steps, each with the number symbol written clearly inside. Show and read each number card, talking about 'o' and where it would be represented. Play some matching games with the numbers. Deal each child a card and ask them to collect the corresponding number of pebbles from a tray and then to go and stand on the correct section of the bridge. Count aloud to check each one. The difficulty of the activity can be varied to suit individuals.

Discussion
Introduce zero by marking where the children stand before reaching the first stone. Count aloud forward and back and then ask: which number comes after one? Which number comes before four? Which number is one more than five? Step and move as they count, and collect pebbles to show number value. Ask: who has more/ who has less?

For younger children
Limit the numbers to low numbers and focus on moving, counting aloud and collecting objects to show number value.

For older children
Help the children write their own chalk symbols and pay more attention to accurate counting and matching.

Follow-up activities
▲ Emphasise counting and comparing by giving each child a target of pebbles to collect.
▲ Blank out one of the steps and ask the children to find the missing number.
▲ Cover a dice with 1–3 red dots and 1–3 green dot. Use it to play the game on photocopiable page 94.
▲ Make sequence bridges with alphabet letters.
  ▲ Extend the bridge to higher numbers.

Sound steps

Objective
Science – to explore sound and how it can be directed or reduced.

Group size
Up to six children.

What you need
Cassette recorder, radio, wind-up toy, alarm clock, percussion instruments, wooden table, junk boxes, blanket, towels, variety of materials and paper.

Preparation
Record some enjoyable music which is of even tone and volume.

What to do
Remind the children of how the goats' trip-trapping sounds alerted the troll. Ask the children to keep still and close their eyes while you play some trip-trap tunes on different percussion instruments. Ask them to guess the source of the sound.

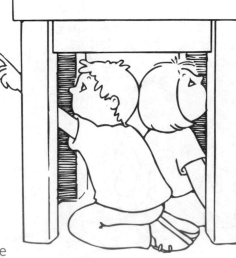

Next ask for volunteer trolls to hide under the table 'bridge' in the middle, with their eyes closed.

Place the radio, tape or toy at one end of the table and ask the troll to point in the direction of the sound. Discuss the quality of the sound and whether it was easy to detect. Repeat, but this time put the sound source in a different position.

Divide the children into groups of two or three and let them take turns at being blindfold trolls or 'sound hiders'. (Ensure they don't alter the volume or type of noise.) Once they have established where the sound is clearest and where it's most difficult to hear, offer them materials to try and 'quieten' the noise. Encourage them to experiment and contrast different types of material such as wrapping the radio in a blanket, or wrapping it in tissue paper.

Discussion
Ask the children to define a noise carefully contrasting loud/soft, high/low and clear/muffled. Use simple directional language to locate sources of sound and to establish how to optimise or reduce it. Ask: where is the radio? Why does it sound loud? Why does it sound muffled?

For younger children
Focus on making clear contrasts between loud and quiet, thick and thin, near and far, in front and behind.

For older children
Let the children design their own tests and develop simple explanations for what and how they're testing sound waves.

Follow-up activities
▲ Explore vibrations using home-made instruments.
▲ Play listening games whereby something has to be moved without waking the troll.
▲ Use reclaimed materials to find shapes which enlarge sound and shapes which reduce it.

Bridge builder

Objective
Design and Technology– to make simple bridges using different materials.

Group size
Four to six children.

What you need
Construction equipment, wooden blocks, play dough, strips of material, reclaimed materials, joining materials – adhesive, sticky tape, string and so on. Scissors. Pictures of different types of bridges. Low stools. Toy cars and toy goats.

What to do
Ask the children to think about the troll's bridge and why we need bridges. Where can they be found? Look together at the different materials and ask the children to select something they think is suitable for building a bridge.

Encourage the children to talk about the properties and suitability of different materials and to describe the problems that they encounter as they work. Ask the children to predict what will happen if you try to spread the material across the two stools to use as a bridge.

Let one group concentrate on using reclaimed materials to build their bridge, focusing on joining, while another group explores bridge structure using construction tools. Give the children opportunities to work with both sets of material and then compare experiences. Encourage the children to evaluate their work throughout, solving problems as they meet them.

Discussion
Ask the children: why didn't the goats choose another route to get to the green grass? Where have you seen bridges? What do they go over and what travels over them? Think of contrasting bridges in your locality and consider what they might be made of.

For younger children
Make bridges with modelling and construction tools. Join three cardboard pieces to form a bridge.

For older children
Encourage co-operative work and experimentation. Encourage the children to think about supporting weight.

Follow-up activities
▲ Make bridge shapes in PE lessons.
▲ Explore a bridge in your local community.
▲ Classify and describe materials which are/are not suitable for making model bridges.
▲ Collect pictures of different bridge designs – comparing shapes, supports and strength.

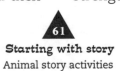

Bridging time

Objective
History – to find out about a local bridge.

Group size
Whole group outing with appropriate adult support.

What you need
Clipboards, pencils, crayons, pictures of contrasting bridges and preferably of your chosen bridge changing over time. Cassette recorder, camera.

Preparation
Research your locality to find a safe bridge with interesting features, preferably of historical interest. Find a viewing spot and a safe place to examine the bridge close-up. Ensure all helpers understand safety rules and learning intentions.

What to do
Look at the pictures of bridges and talk about why they were built, who uses them and so on. Are any children familiar with your chosen bridge? If so, encourage them to share their experiences. Explain the purpose of your visit and give firm safety and behaviour instructions. Once you reach the 'viewing spot', note the shape of the bridge, its purpose, how frequently it is being used and so on.

Make sketches, take photos and record comments made by the children. Take some rubbings of the bridge and try to view it from varying angles. Think about its size and shape, about the noises associated with it and take some tape recordings. Talk about changes in transport and in the immediate environment, so the children appreciate something of the bridge's history. Encourage them to spot any clues about the bridge's past. Finally, take a photo of something newer than the bridge, the bridge itself and, if appropriate, something older than the bridge.

Discussion
Ask the children to think of as many types of transport as they can. How did people travel around before cars? Look at the shape and size of your bridge and guess what it's made of. Is it particularly high or long, does it move and what travels beneath it? Show the children where to look for changes in the structure and other interesting clues about its past.

For younger children
Concentrate on the purpose of the bridge and on contrasting old and new developments in the location. Keep it simple and show how your recordings provide a record of what the bridge is like *now*.

For older children
Relate what you see to ideas of change and development through a key event such as flooding/widening/a railway line closing in the past. Talk in more detail about transport and show the children old photos in reference books.

Follow-up activities
▲ Find out about famous bridges.
▲ Use your sketches and photos to make a collage of the bridge. Invite older children to contrast past and present transport over the bridge.
▲ Make an annotated collection of the children's favourite bridges.

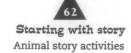

Graze your goat

Objective
Geography – to appreciate different types of land use.

Group size
Up to six children.

What you need
Playmats, toy cars, trains, animals and houses. Aerial photos of the local community. Paper and drawing materials. Toy goat puppets.

What to do
Remind the children about why the goats wanted to cross the troll's bridge. Ask the children if they have ever seen a real goat and gather ideas about the needs and habitats of goats. Help the children understand differences between open and urban space, natural and man-made, transport and recreation areas.

Let the children play with the mats and toys before asking them to arrange all the cars and animals into appropriate locations. Look at and discuss the different options chosen by the children.

Use bought or made puppets to role-play an anxious goat who asks for the children's help in finding a safe place to stay. Ask the children to draw and talk about their ideas for the goat.

Discussion
Ask the children to talk about where they feel safe to play, where they eat and where they rest. Discuss dangerous spaces such as roads and railways and places built for relaxing like playgrounds. Use your goat character to discuss where there is plenty of grass, who uses the land and whether it is safe from traffic. Ask the children whether they know anyone who keeps goats and how they are cared for.

For younger children
Use the opportunity to introduce simple geographical terms to these children. Help them to understand terms such as river, field and town.

For older children
Think about man-made landscapes such as towns, roads and railways. Contrast these with commons, woods, parks and open spaces.

Follow-up activities
▲ Look at goats on a real farm.
▲ Produce guides to safe places to play and identify spots where it would be very dangerous.
▲ Take the opportunity to teach the road safety drill, what to do when out shopping, and other personal safety tips.

Terrible troll models

Objective
Art – to explore clay modelling.

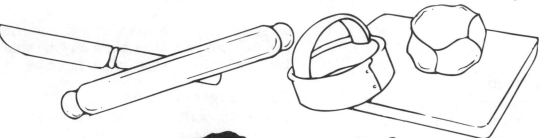

Group size
Up to six children.

What you need
A large tennis-ball sized lump of clay for each child, boards, water, cleaning materials, aprons, shaping tools.

What to do
Discuss the troll's appearance and size, explaining that the children are each going to make a clay model.

Give them plenty of time to feel and mould the clay, enjoying the tactile experience.

Let them try rolling the lump and changing its shape. Can they make the surface smooth and then rough? Now encourage them to roll the clay into a solid lump and to each think about the body shape of their monster.

Ask the children to let head and arm features 'grow' out of the body. Use tools to draw on the features and to experiment with texture. Focus on letting the children explore and relish the experience of clay before leaving any finished trolls to dry.

Watch how the clay changes as it dries and try buffing up the surface with the back of a spoon at the 'leather hard' stage.

Discussion
Ask the children about the colour and feel of clay. How heavy and solid does it feel, is it cold and hard, is it smooth to touch? They will need to get used to the texture of the clay and learn how it behaves in a different way to dough when moulded, squeezed and poked. Help them to describe each experience and observe the shapes they make.

For younger children
Allow the children to enjoy the feel of the clay, concentrating on its consistency and ways to mould it using their hands. How many different ways can they change it?

For older children
Allow the children to experiment with making different shapes. Encourage them to try joining using slip to smooth it and to avoid cracking when drying. When they have finished their trolls let them add details using twigs and so on.

Follow-up activities
▲ Use different modelling media to create a variety of monster trolls.
▲ Make a clay bridge for your troll to live under.
▲ Dress up as terrible trolls and do a 'Hopping Mad Dance'.

Bell and hoof trot

Objective
Music – to appreciate different tempo and to make percussion instruments.

Group size
Up to six children.

What you need
Wooden sticks, claves, castanets, cymbals, variety of drums. Plastic tubs and containers with lids, cardboard tubes, dried pasta/peas/rice of different sizes, scissors, sticky and masking tape, adhesive, rubber bands (ensure close supervision). Paper and pens.

What to do
Enjoy re-living the 'bridge-crossing' section of the story, choosing 'goats' and 'trolls' and emphasising contrasts in their 'trip-trap' noises.

Using one finger tap the hoof beat. Build up to four fingers and then loud claps, trapping air with rounded hands.

Now use hand movements to create three goat characters, describing changes in speed, volume and tone.

Let the children listen to and then sample different instruments. Ask for volunteers to select appropriate sounds for the goats. Can the children make their instrument 'change' to reflect two of the goats? Finally, select pots or tubes and fill with small or large-grained material to make a 'shaker' for each child. Decorate the shakers and play them in your trained 'Goat Orchestra'!

Discussion
Ask how the troll could guess who was coming onto his bridge. When using hands, ask them how the sounds change, whether they are hard or soft, loud or quiet. Ask the children to show you one of the goats with their instrument and then ask: how are you playing? Are your beats fast or slow, heavy or light?

For younger children
Let younger children concentrate on good listening skills by learning to copy a sound quality. Encourage them to appreciate the strong contrasts in sound.

For older children
Allow more freedom and much greater experimentation in instrument design. Encourage the children to consider differing quantities of filling and different types of material for lids or covers.

Follow-up activities
▲ Make up simple rhythms for each goat to travel across the bridge.
▲ Add drama by inventing troll music with fierce clashes and sudden bangs.
▲ Make up songs based on the text each goat would use going over the bridge.
▲ Make recordings of children's work to play back and interpret like a guessing game.

Bridge balances

Objective
PE – to explore different ways of balancing and making bridge shapes.

Group size
Whole group.

What you need
Three contrasting percussion instruments and a cymbal. Mats.

What to do
Explain to the children that they are going to move around the room like the three Billy Goats Gruff. Ask the children to find a space and to slowly fold up and stay completely still. Listen to the light, quick sound made on a percussion instrument and think which goat it could represent. Now leap up and dart around the room shaking horns, hooves and tails. At the sound of the troll's crashing cymbal, freeze and try to hold the shape. Notice which balances are easy to hold and which are more challenging, praising variety, creativity and attempts at control.

Now think about a balance that would make a good bridge shape and hold it carefully. Add the instruments now in a moving and balancing game, asking the children to prance around in the correct goat character. On hearing the troll's crash, they transform into a bridge statue until the troll goes back to sleep. Encourage a new bridge shape each time. Finish by slowly folding up as bridges and moving back in a stiff, stone-like manner.

Discussion
Ask: which parts of your body are easy to move fast? What parts of your body are you balanced on? Is it a small or large part? Is yours a high or low bridge? What happens to your balance as you make your bridge wider or narrower?

For younger children
Focus on making good simple balances. Demonstrate balances on small and large body parts and ask the children to try and copy them.

For older children
Think more closely about the skill of balancing. What is involved in finding ways to hold a shape without moving? Demonstrate bridge shapes by arching and lowering your back.

Follow-up activities
▲ Make bridge shapes over small and large quoits.
▲ Test out the stability of balances by using bean bags balanced on heads.
▲ Find some different ways to move and travel around in any way other than on your feet.
▲ Take photos of successful bridge balances and ask other children to describe how they are achieved.

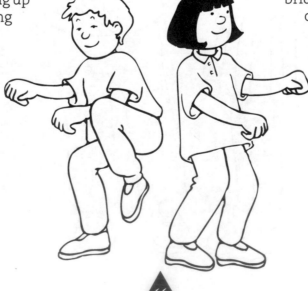

Big bully

Objective
RE – to discuss problems of bullying. To consider practical strategies together.

Group size
Up to six children.

What you need
Two old plain socks for each child, scissors, adhesive, needle and thread, felt pieces, material and wool, felt-tipped pens, buttons.

What to do
Discuss the way the troll behaved, what reasons he might have had and how he made the goats feel. Think of times when the children have felt sad, frightened or unhappy because of the way someone behaved towards them. Help the children to express their feelings, learn how to get help, how to talk things through to find better ways of working and playing together. Focus on shared responsibility not individual blame.

Make some puppet characters together using the socks and other materials, with one terrible troll face and one terrific happy troll. Help the children to choose appropriate materials create the features and personality. Invent a scenario, such as playing with construction toys and ask the children to use the puppets to show how 'nice' and 'nasty' trolls would behave! Finish by re-enacting a different version of the story where the troll helps each goat over his bridge and invites them to tea!

Discussion
Talk about what it feels like to be bullied, helping them describe times they have been made unhappy but *without* mentioning names. (Explain this is because you want *all* the children to help in preventing bullying.) Ask: how does a bully act? What do they say? How do they look? Ask whether bullies mean to upset you, why they act that way and how it makes them feel. Talk about how to get help, to share your feelings and to find solutions, relating this to behaviour programmes.

For younger children
Use your puppet characters to create a familiar context for the children to discuss. Concentrate on appreciating the difference between right and wrong.

For older children
Give the children more scope to make up their own dialogue and to apply their own experiences.

Follow-up activities
▲ Make a giant troll with a letterbox mouth, who swallows tips on how to behave.
▲ Make up agreed rules for avoiding bullying and for seeking help.
▲ Make a 'Kind Kid' goat badge for rewarding positive and caring kinds of behaviour.

The trip-trap bridge

river collage

four posts

six planks with different textures

thick string or rope

grey/brown rocks

lush green grass

What you need

Six flat and lightweight planks, thick string, adhesive for wood and paper. Nails and hammer, thick string. Four sticks (same size and safe). Blue, green and grey backing paper. Scraps of blue, green, grey, paper – shiny, transparent and so on. Paints – brown/green and so on. Sandpaper, pasta, egg boxes, bark chip, velvet, plastic packing bubbles and foil (no sharp edges). Scissors, newspaper, toy goats and paper.

Preparation

Use a low display space so that children can feel the different textures which will cover each plank. Put up backing paper for sky, one side of a steep canyon with grey backing paper, the other green. Saw planks to create a curved bridge which will fit your display space.

What to do

Look at the display board and agree which is the grassy side and which the rocky one. Protect the floor and then let the children paint on rocks and grass, perhaps adding other features and clouds/sun. Use the scraps of paper to create a fast-flowing river. Ask the children how the goats crossed over, then show them the six planks. Help them to select from the range of materials and cover each plank to create a different texture and sound. Decorate where necessary. Then, using the thick string or rope, plus nails, fasten the planks to the wall to create a feely rope bridge. Tie the ends to your four posts. (Characters can be added if necessary but keep the bridge clear for 'walking' over.) Encourage the children to describe each plank and to listen to contrasting sounds as the toy goats 'walk' over the bridge.

Discussion

Look at the display and remind the children of the story, asking: why do the goats want to leave this side? How will they get to this lush green grass? Ask how the bridge could be built – which planks go together? How will the planks be secured?

Follow-up activities

▲ Make a display table of construction kits and challenge the children to build bridges.
▲ Make up musical journeys in keeping with the sounds or feel of each plank.

Goats

Three Billy-Goats Gruff

hard and strong black/brown

bell

key features as collage

grass

white and orange/brown

soft and fluffy white/cream

What you need

Thick paint in three goat shades, combs, variety of brushes, beads, buttons, cotton reels. Reclaimed material, scraps of wool and fabric. Backing paper in shades of green, sugar paper, scissors, adhesive, crayons.

Preparation

Put up backing paper and cut sugar paper to three appropriate goat sizes.

What to do

Let the children decide which colour would suit each sized goat and then select printing materials to make furry lines (combs, fingers, brushes, swirling movements) all over your goat outlines on the sugar paper. Leave to dry. Look at the reclaimed materials – beads, buttons, reels and fabric scraps, to decide how features are to be added. Show the children how to twist paper into horns and talk about appropriate shapes and textures. Encourage the children to make goats with clearly different identities, colours and textures.

Carefully mount each one on the grassy background. Add green grass for one of them to chew, flowers near another and perhaps a bell for the third. Use the opportunity to extend positional language and to retell the story.

Discussion

Ask the children what they know about real goats, and to describe the character of each goat in the story. Ask: what special things must we add to show this is a goat? What shape should the horns be? What could we use to make the beard/the hooves/the tail? Whose fur would be the softest/fluffiest/thickest? When the display is up, ask them about the size and appearance of each goat.

Follow-up activities

▲ Collect goat stories and picture books for display.
▲ Use toy goats of different colours for sorting, matching and counting activities.
▲ Have a texture display, contrasting hard/soft, smooth/bumpy and so on.

Green grass pasta

Group size
Four to six children.

What you need
Kitchen knives and chopping boards, two large saucepans, grater, spoons, wooden spoon, fork, tin opener, plates and colander. Aprons, washing up equipment. Ingredients: 1 onion, 1 of each red/green pepper, water, courgettes, 150g mushrooms, 1 tablespoon olive oil, seasoning, 400g canned tomatoes, 1 teaspoon mixed herbs, 2 tablespoons tomato puree, 100g cheese, 250g pasta verde.

What to do
Ensure children understand safety rules and demonstrate chopping techniques carefully. First chop the onion, noting how this can affect the eyes. Chop other vegetables carefully. Brown onions in some oil, then add the courgettes, mushrooms and pepper. Cook gently for five minutes. Remove from the heat so children can add tinned tomatoes, puree, mixed herbs and seasoning. Bring to the boil, then lower heat and leave to simmer for 30 minutes, stirring occasionally. Now half-fill the

other saucepan with water, add salt and a drop of oil and bring to the boil. Look at the dry pasta, describe its feel and taste. Put it carefully in the boiling water but allow the children to observe changes from a distance. Simmer for ten minutes before showing the children how to test the pasta. Wash up while you are waiting and grate the cheese. Let the children watch how you drain the pasta, and leave to cool slightly before adding to the vegetables and sprinkling with grated cheese to serve.

Discussion
Talk about the way ingredients change when heated. Ask about shape, colour and texture plus smell and taste. Why do some things need cooking before eating? Discuss safety rules for chopping and general care when cooking. Notice steam and noises associated with boiling and simmering.

Follow-up activities
▲ Experiment with different types of pasta.
▲ Have a green vegetable display and try different ways of cooking them.
▲ Use dried pasta for floating and sinking experiments, explore their shapes closely.

The Town Mouse and the Country Mouse

This delightful tale focuses on our need for security and the reassurance of familiar surroundings. Coping with change is fundamental to modern life and so the tale has great topical appeal. We also learn how town and country environments differ. The tale encourages empathy and tolerance and allows exploration of these themes at different levels.

There were once two mice who were cousins, one lived in the country and one lived in a town. One day, Town Mouse decided to visit her cousin in the country. It was a long bumpy journey in the back of a market van. When she arrived, Town Mouse wasn't happy with the straw bundle her cousin invited her to rest on and she was disappointed when he offered her a few berries topped with seed for tea. She didn't want to upset her cousin, so she agreed to go for a stroll. But she had never seen such a muddy path – there were no pavements and lights or shops to look in! She froze with fear as an owl swooped down, attracted by her bright coat. The two mice fled home. What an awful night poor Town Mouse had! Town Mouse couldn't sleep because the straw was too uncomfortable and the night too silent and still.

The next day, Town Mouse packed her case and said sorry to her cousin, 'The country's just not for me. Come back with me and see how comfy life can be'.

The journey was a nightmare for Country Mouse. He had never been in a bumpy, noisy van, nor seen such traffic, heard such sounds or smelled such smells. Country Mouse felt quite sick and dizzy.

At last they reached Town Mouse's home where just as they were about to go under the stairs a big furry shadow blocked their way. A cat! Country Mouse froze and only escaped from those terrible claws as his cousin dragged him under the sofa. Town Mouse put her cousin to bed and gave him lots of rich food that upset his tummy. Country Mouse lay awake all night listening to voices, music and distant traffic, his nose twitching with the smells of humans and cats.

The next morning he said sorry to his cousin, 'I have to go home, the town terrifies me. I'm sorry my dear, but I'll write to you soon'.

So Country Mouse returned to his own sweet home, and Town Mouse remained in hers. And although they wrote often, neither wanted to leave their safe, happy homes again.

I'm feeling

Objective
English – to encourage children to explore and express their feelings.

Group size
Up to six children.

What you need
Card, scissors, string, drawing or collage materials. White board. Hole punch. Copy of the story.

Preparation
Cut card into appropriate sizes for making face masks. Ensure you are aware of any sensitive home situations.

What to do
Re-tell the story. Focus on how each mouse feels in his or her own environment, extending language beyond 'happy' to consider ideas such as 'relaxed' and 'proud'. Relate this to the children's own experience of feeling secure. Now contrast this with how the mice felt away from home, again drawing out the children's descriptive language. Recent visits or having to join in something new, will help the children relate their own experiences.

Encourage the children to role-play each mouse's experience, with their emotions turning to fear, anxiety and loneliness in unfamiliar surroundings. Then help each child make a two-sided mouse mask, with ties for fastening. Model contrasting facial expressions so that the mouse looks happy and relaxed on one side, and worried and concerned on the other. Decorate and give each 'mouse' a turn at expressing their positive and negative emotions.

Discussion
Share your own experiences when facing change, describing how you felt and why. Use mouse role-play to extend language by asking: how does your mouse feel? When do you feel like that? Where are you and what are you doing? (Help the children draw parallels with their own experiences, but be sensitive to individual circumstances.) Help with non-verbal communication, modelling appropriate face and body movements.

For younger children
Focus on mouse role-play and strong contrasts, before helping cut and decorate the masks. Use elasticated thread and help take masks on and off.

For older children
Consider the causes and consequences of each emotion in greater depth, such as how each mouse faced up to his or her feelings and found a solution.

Follow-up activities
▲ Make a 'Feeling at home' booklet to celebrate familiar routines.
▲ Encourage role-play in your home corner, contrasting situations when we are at home to times when we go and visit somebody else in their home.
▲ Make finger and glove puppets to retell the story and develop your own versions.
▲ Read stories such as *Moving Molly* by Shirley Hughes (Red Fox) to encourage further discussion about moving house.

Pack your bags!

Objective
English – to develop auditory and visual sequential memory.

Group size
Up to six children.

What you need
Small suitcase or bag, clothes, toiletries and other 'travel' items.

Preparation
Check there is a logical range of items and a manageable number to remember.

What to do
Discuss what Town Mouse might have packed in his case before setting off to visit his cousin. Encourage the children to talk about when they have gone on holiday or to stay somewhere. Ask them to think about what things they have to take and which special things, such as their favourite soft toys, they like to take.

Now look at your suitcase and invite the children to describe and order the items inside. Explain that they are going to play 'listening and looking' memory games as they pack the case. Form a circle around the items and ask each child to take a turn at saying: 'I packed my case and I took..' adding one item to a cumulative sequence. Point to each object being chosen to aid memory and concentration. Repeat the game, this time putting each chosen item in the bag. Then play a 'looking' memory game, laying out three to four items to be packed and describing them in order from left to right.

Pack the items away and take turns at naming them before setting them out again in the correct order. Allow free play before asking the children to devise their own memory games, modelling positive social skills.

Discussion
Name and describe each item, asking: why do we need to pack it? Ask the children to group items according to how and when they're used. Talk about times the children have stayed away from home, contrasting holiday packing with an overnight trip to Gran's. Ask the children about things they need to pack or remember to do each morning and talk through the sequence, using ordinal terms.

For younger children
Restrict the number of items so that all can build on success.

For older children
Increase the items and the complexity, with greater emphasis on how to remember items in the correct order.

Follow-up activities
▲ Draw picture sequences of holiday items and play matching, copying and remembering games with them.
▲ Encourage role-play activities which require remembering shopping items and instructions in sequence.
▲ Use a cassette for some listening memory games – repeat back a list then replay to check.

Show me the way

Objective
Mathematics – to practise using directional and positional terms.

Group size
Up to six children.

What you need
Photocopiable page 95, paper, drawing materials, white board, playmats, toy cars, mice and so on. Magnetic figure. Copy of the story.

Preparation
Photocopy sheet 95 for each child.

What to do
Ask the children about Mouse's journey to and from town. Help them use illustrations to relate the journey in sequence and enrich their description with appropriate terms such as along, over and across.

Talk about daily journeys the children make, selecting ones with which they are all familiar. Then use the white board to draw on a simple route including features such as a park, shop and crossroads, starting from 'home' and ending at an agreed destination such as 'school'. Use your magnetic figure to 'walk and talk' the journey. Introduce terms such as 'corner' and 'along'. Repeat the exercise with children taking turns to 'walk' the figure and then invite the children to 'talk' a journey for you to follow.

Show the children the sheet, describe the details and talk through all the instructions. Locate the start and finish and support each child as they draw on and describe a route for Mouse to follow.

Discussion
Ask the children questions about the journeys they make: when you leave your house to come here, do you go up or down the road? Do you go right or left? Do you walk straight or do you turn a corner? Use real objects, short walks and the drawings to reinforce a few new terms.

For younger children
Keep it simple, introducing opposites such as 'over and under' one at a time. Allow plenty of free play with real objects and real walks around the room.

For older children
Let the children experiment and set more complex journeys with two to three positional opposites. Teach them how to practise 'right' and 'left' using hand orientation and clues.

Follow-up activities
▲ Draw little maps of regular routes around your building. Describe them accurately.
▲ Work with a partner, one driving and the other directing a route around the playmat.
▲ Create a display of positional terms for the children to illustrate. Make Velcro copies of each word so they can detach them and demonstrate their understanding.

Pack and match

Objective
Mathematics – to reinforce one-to-one correspondence and comparative language.

Group size
Six to eight children.

What you need
Two sets of cases, doll's clothing, food and items which can be readily distinguished as belonging to 'smart' town mouse or 'simple' country mouse. An extra hat and shoes for Town Mouse. Two toy mice dressed to match the characters. A copy of the story. Card and pen.

What to do
Go through the story identifying sections relating to the town and those relating to the country. Introduce the toy mice and encourage the children to describe their appearance and character. Tell the children that the mice need to pack their bags for their visits.

Ask the children to find each mouse a suitable bag. Then sort through the clothing, food and bedding, deciding whether they belong to Town or Country Mouse. (For example, Town Mouse might rest on a cushion whereas Country Mouse might have a pile of straw.) Arrange the items so that the children can readily match and compare the objects and it is visually clear that Town Mouse has two extra items. Let the children guess which mouse has more and which has fewer before counting each set into the appropriate bag. Then ask the children to check back, matching each item to establish what Town Mouse has more of. Write out labels 'more' and 'fewer', fixing them to the right case.

Discussion
Talk about the purpose or name of each item and ask: can you find its partner? Ask the children to give reasons for choosing particular items for each mouse. Ask: which mouse has more things in their case? Which has fewer? How many things does Town Mouse have? What does he have more of?

For younger children
Limit the number and type of objects so that they can be clearly matched. Add one hat to distinguish more/ less totals.

For older children
Encourage the children to sort the items more independently. Ask them to find a matching or similar object, so the extra items are obvious. Let them decide where to place the 'more' and 'fewer' labels and ask them to explain their reasons.

Follow-up activities
▲ Make a large collage comparing the belongings of each mouse.
▲ Let the children sort and re-sort town or country photos.
▲ Make a simple matching game with drawings of mice and woollen tails to be stuck on.
▲ Use round red beads to count Country Mouse's berries and yellow cubes to count Town Mouse's cheese. Compare the two results.

Can you smell danger?

Objective
Science – to develop awareness of sensory perception, particularly smell.

Group size
Up to six children.

What you need
Range of six smells – lavender, thyme, eucalyptus, onion, coffee, dried herbs, food flavourings, cotton wool. 12 small plastic pots, clear plastic film, needle. Selection of cheeses, sweets or jellies, small plastic plates, cleaning equipment.

Preparation
Make two cotton wool swabs for each smell, secure them in pots which are covered with clear plastic film. Pierce plenty of holes. Cut up chunks of cheese and arrange a selection on each plate.

What to do
Remind the children of the real and imagined dangers faced by the mice, discussing how the mice anticipated them. Consider with the children how our senses help alert us to danger. The children will readily think about sight and sound, now help them to focus in on their other senses.

Ask the children to pretend to be cautious mice creeping around the room and mimic mice sniffing to smell whether there's a cat or cheese around the corner! Let your 'mice' sniff a cheese sample each and try to describe it. Now play a sniffing guessing game with your covered pots, insisting that the children hold the pot some way away. (Establish clear hygiene rules). Ask your 'mice detectives' to smell each pot carefully so that the matching pot can be found. Finally offer a small sweet, asking each child to close their eyes and guess the flavour by smell before tasting it.

Discussion
Ask the children: how can we tell if we might be in danger? How would we know about a fire or being near a busy road? How could we tell if we shouldn't eat something? Ask the children to describe some of their favourite and least favourite smells.

For younger children
Focus on just two contrasting smells and upon the dangers and delights that we sense through smell.

For older children
Encourage the children to work co-operatively to find the matching pairs. Record or scribe their descriptions and then try to match these back to the correct scent.

Follow-up activities
▲ Make a 'smelly collection' and produce a graph of likes and dislikes.
▲ Go on a scent trail, contrasting natural and man-made scents.
▲ Design safety posters which show how smell can alert us to potential dangers.

Welcome home mouse!

Objective
Design and Technology – to select materials to make a simple bag.

Group size
Four to six children.

What you need
Reclaimed materials, including boxes cut in half, plastic containers and cardboard tubes. Masking and sticky tape, adhesive, scissors, string, card, material. Decorating materials, pencils and paper. Pictures and samples of cases, bags and so on.

What to do
Using the story as a starting point, discuss experiences of packing and travelling. Look at the pictures to discuss different types of bags for different purposes. Identify common features and think about how they serve the purpose of transporting items. Help the children identify materials used to make different bags and to decide which are particularly strong. Look at the range of materials, discussing types, shapes and forms.

Explain to the children that you want them to make a bag for the Mouse to pack. Ask each child to sketch out their ideas, to collect useful materials and to decide how parts will be joined, before starting to make their bag. Encourage them to test out their designs and to agree upon suitable permanent joins before decorating and leaving for Mouse to fill.

Discussion
Ask the children when they use bags, how they carry books, shopping, picnics and so on. Ask: what part of the bag do you hold? What part of the bag supports your things? Why don't your things fall out? Explore vocabulary such as: handles, straps, zips, sides and bottoms of bags. Describe the shapes of different bags and agree upon a useful but realistic size for the bags you make for Mouse.

For younger children
Let the children experiment with pre-cut boxes, and help them design simple handles. Offer support with cutting and securing to ensure success.

For older children
Encourage careful planning and a review of how successful their ideas were. Offer a wider range of materials and joining equipment.

Follow-up activities
▲ Leave the bags for Mouse to magically fill and write a thank you letter for.
▲ Explore fastenings and help the children learn how to use a zip.
▲ Make a collection of different bags and cases, and use as a basis for a luggage shop.

Moving on

Objective
History – to develop an appreciation of personal history and chronology.

Group size
Six to eight children.

What you need
Thin card, colouring materials and pencils. Selection of family photos showing holiday scenes. Estate agents' adverts and books about journeys and moving.

Preparation
Cut and fold card to make a six-page concertina booklet for each child.

What to do
Think about how each mouse felt before their visit, contrasting it with how they felt at the end of the story. Ask the children to consider recent changes they have experienced. These may be very varied, from those children who have moved home, to staying with a relative or friend. (Be sensitive to individual children's circumstances.)

Ask the children to think of a trip or journey they have made. To start with ask them to think about the anticipation before a journey including the preparation that is necessary. Then ask them to think how they felt after the event. Try to establish an awareness of change, from learning new skills to making new friends and so on.

Help the children explore these changes by creating 'before and after' or 'now and then' booklets. Ask the children to think of an example of how they felt before and after their chosen experience. They should then draw a 'before' picture on one side and

an 'after' picture on the other. Encourage the children to share their illustrated booklets afterwards.

Discussion
Ask the children to recall trips away from home and ask: how did you feel? What did you do to get ready? What did you take with you? Now help the children to consider how they felt afterwards: what did you bring home? What new things did you do? Who did you meet? How did you feel to be back at home? Let them feel a sense of achievement in making these adjustments and learning from the positive benefits of change.

For younger children
Concentrate on simple before and after contrasts and on helping the children celebrate their achievements as they change and grow.

For older children
Help the children to draw parallels between their experiences and to see the learning benefits of the changes they experience.

Follow-up activities
▲ Make journey maps out of pictures to show a sequence of events before, during and after a special trip.
▲ Make props for 'journey' role-play, encouraging children to talk through anxieties.
▲ Collect postcards and photographs to build up a gallery of past experiences.
▲ Choose a familiar local journey to illustrate a sequence of events.

Town or country?

Objective
Geography – to understand the differences between town and rural locations.

Group size
Four to eight children.

What you need
Photocopiable sheet 96, paper, copy of the story, pictures and/or books of town or country scenes, drawing materials. White board and markers.

What to do
Flip through the books, using the illustrations to gather contrasts of town and country scenery. Use the white board to scribe key words and ideas raised by the children, helping them to focus on the types and density of housing, roads, shops and other services compared with open fields and woodland.

Now think about your own locality. Look out of the window or, if possible, take the children outside so that they can assess whether you are in a town – is there lots of housing, or are you near a busy road or close to shops? Listen for noises and, without leaving the grounds, observe traffic and passers by.

Return to your room and work through the photocopiable classification sheet, as a group. Turn the sheet over and ask the children to draw their own home. Support each child in turn as they define their location and then think of clue words like 'lots of cars', 'opposite a farm' or 'no street lights', to support their choice.

Discussion
Ask the children to describe each mouse's home and the types of noises and sights that fit with either town or country. Invite the children to describe their journey to school. Prompt them by asking them to tell you about the houses they see, what traffic is on the roads. Ask: do you pass open fields and woods? Where do you go to play? Ask where the nearest shops, trains and sports centre are. Ask: what can you see from your bedroom window?

For younger children
Help make simple connections, using housing, street size and the proximity of a big shopping centre as clues.

For older children
Consider the locality in more depth. Is the open space an urban park? How many houses are in their street? How near are they to churches, shops and other services? How many people do they pass on the way to school?

Follow-up activities
▲ Make a collage of town and country landscapes, labelling with key differences.
▲ Make a sorting display of town and country words and pictures.
▲ Produce booklets about the local area for people who live in very different locations.
▲ Celebrate the diversity of your locality.

Pop-up mouse

Objective
Art – to use simple paper craft to make a pop-up character.

Group size
Up to six children.

What you need
Two A4 pieces of thin card for each child, scissors, pencils and decorating materials.

Preparation
Fold one of each pair of A4 card in half (base) and cut the other into A5 pieces. Fold one A5 piece in half and cut a diagonal section off the corner. Fold down flaps. Once the mouse characters are drawn, glue onto the base as shown below.

What to do
Discuss how anxious the mice were away from home at night. Invite the children to pretend that they are the sleeping mice and ask them to wake up startled as you make town or country night noises.

Show the children a sample pop-up. Ask them to design a pop-up scared mouse card by drawing a bed base (A4 sheet) and a frightened mouse character (A5 sheet). Talk to the children and encourage them to use bold and accurate colouring, adding detail.

Once the bed covers and mice have been drawn, help the children with the process of making a pop-up – letting them help, if possible, with cutting round the mouse and with sticking the flaps onto the decorated bed base. Close the flap, admiring the 'surprise' as you open up each in turn.

Discussion
Ask the children about their mouse: how does your mouse show that he's scared? Invite the children to talk about the features which distinguish whether they have drawn Town or Country Mouse, and about the types of bedding, straw, duvets, blankets and so on, that each mouse might have. Ask the children to point to the front and back, top and bottom of their base card. Help them to locate the middle fold and describe your actions as you position and stick each flap.

For younger children
Simply experiment with bold, exciting colouring and do the cutting and sticking craft for the children, describing the process as you do so.

For older children
Encourage the children to find shapes which suit the pop-up style. Talk about balance and colour contrasts. Let the children take a more active part in the whole paper craft.

Follow-up activities
▲ Use other paper craft methods such as flaps, folds and concertinas to make individual 'Mouse story books'.
▲ Make a collection of favourite stories which use these techniques.
▲ Create oral stories and 'speech bubbles' for the pop-up characters.

1. Fold an A4 sheet in half. Decorate it like a bed.

2. Take an A5 piece of paper. Fold in half as shown.

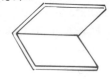

3. Draw on mouse shape. Cut off corner and fold back tabs. Add on thread, whiskers and features.

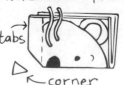

tabs

corner

4. Put glue on tabs and place on top of A4 sheet at the angle shown.

glue

Sounds familiar

Objective
Music – to develop listening skills and to distinguish between types of sound.

Group size
Any size is suitable.

What you need
Cassette recorder, cassette, sources of environmental noise or sound effect tape. Evocative music such as *First Cuckoo in Spring* by Delius and Beethoven's *Pastoral No. 6*, compared with Vaughan Williams' *London Symphony* and Grace Jones' 'Roll up to the Bumper...'. Whistles, cymbals, coconut shells, wooden sticks, claves, castanets, variety of drums.

Preparation
Record three 'town' sounds, such as traffic noise, a busy market and lots of commuters leaving a train station. Contrast this with owl and country night noises, such as a tractor and farm animals.

What to do
With the children go outside and listen carefully to noises around you. Ask the children to describe the different types of noises and to guess their source. Return indoors and play the sound effects tape which should contain three of each contrasting noise. Let the children identify the noises and their likely location.

Discuss whether there is more than one sound at a time, whether it is continuous, loud or soft and so on. Encourage the children to mimic the noises with their voices and help them to focus on any patterns and repetition in the sounds.

Now listen to the two different types of music, asking the children to shut their eyes and then to describe what they 'see'.

Encourage accuracy and detail, linking the sound to objects, such as cars, or to moods, such as still and peaceful. Finally, use voices and then instruments to make up town or country contrasts for other children to interpret.

Discussion
Ask: what is making that sound? Is there one sound or lots of sounds? What is the loudest sound/the highest sound/the longest sound? Ask the children to clap to show when the noise starts and finishes and to use their hands to indicate when it rises or falls.

For younger children
Concentrate on good listening skills to appreciate different sounds and the sound qualities of 'loud and soft' or 'fast and slow'.

For older children
Encourage greater sophistication of listening skills, with more subtle contrasts and patterns being explored. Allow time for these children to develop and create their own musical performance.

Follow-up activities
▲ Play a lotto game using different everyday sounds.
▲ Create movements and a dance to accompany the different styles of sound.
▲ Add contrasting sound effects to support a Town Mouse and Country Mouse drama.

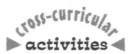

Mouse maps

Objective
PE – to explore ways of travelling and to respond to signals.

Group size
Whole group.

What you need
Whistle, cymbals.

What to do
Ask the children to find a space and to warm up, using different body parts. Contrast fast and slow body movements and different directions without actually travelling.

Now remind the children of how the mice had a hectic journey to town, the dangers they encountered and the things they had to dart and dodge. Tell the children to move in straight lines, using small, fast but controlled movements. Link this to mice darting up and down roads. Repeat, but this time finding ways of travelling low down and then high up. Look for positive examples to show a range of straight, purposeful movements.

Next introduce the whistle, linking it to the mice in the centre of town having to constantly dodge and change direction. Ask the children to travel in a straight line and, when they hear the whistle, to change direction and alter the way they are travelling. When the children are confident with this introduce the cymbals as a signal to 'freeze'. Finally, cool down by stretching out on 'mouse' beds, curling limbs and muscles as the 'mice' relax in slumber.

Discussion
Describe ways of moving in a straight line, starting with walking. Ask: which body parts are you using to balance? Are you travelling high or low? How do you manage to move in a straight line? Let the children consider how they can make fine, sharp movements and build in mouse-like qualities to their work.

For younger children
Focus on using space efficiently, exploring ways of travelling safely avoiding other children. Model two to three examples for the children to copy.

For older children
Think more closely about the skill and quality of ways of travelling, focusing on specific positions, such as high and low. Encourage them to build up to a sequence of two to three movements using whistle and cymbal cues.

Follow-up activities
▲ Make musical pathways to accompany your movements.
▲ Take 'journey and routes' as a theme and paint or draw maps to show your movements.
▲ Make maps and dances as representations of regular journeys which the children take and with which they are familiar.

Welcome!

Objective
RE – to explore ways of caring and of showing hospitality.

Group size
Up to six children.

What you need
Home corner role-play area, biscuits, plastic plates, cups and saucers, juice.

What to do
Discuss how each mouse tried to make his or her guest feel comfortable and happy. Think about special things they might have done and relate them to the children's own experiences. Think of a time a relative or friend has been to stay or visit. Describe the catering, cleaning, caring and planning before that guest arrived. Role-play these experiences, acting as a model to extend language and enrich the children's play. Focus on how you might greet a guest and what you would do to make them feel at home and refreshed. Again, act out these ideas together. Encourage empathy for a guest, ask them to think of any feelings of tiredness and anxiety they might have and gather suggestions of how this might be relieved. Ask the children to prepare their home corner for a special guest, thinking about making beds, tidying up and setting out the juice and biscuits. Take turns at being either the hosts or the guests. Finish by asking the children to think about which things made them feel good and which things made their 'guests' feel welcome.

Discussion
Talk about what it feels like to visit somewhere. Ask: how do you make Grandma or a friend feel special? What do you do to help them if they are tired or hungry? What things make them feel happy? How do you help them feel at home? Talk about what you put out, make or buy and how you might need to share beds, toys or bathroom space so that your guest is happy.

For younger children
Use the role-play experience to help the children appreciate the need to think of others and how signs of caring make visitors happy.

For older children
Give the children opportunities to think more closely about people's individual needs. Ask them to think about how they might have to change their own personal routines.

Follow-up activities
▲ Follow up the children's 'special' suggestions such as making a card, a cake or arranging flowers.
▲ Compile a list of how new children should be welcomed by the group.
▲ Make 'Helpful Host' badges to reward positive caring behaviour.

Town or country?

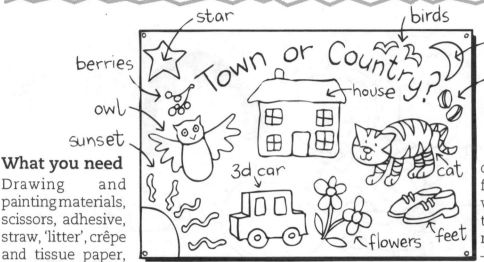

What you need

Drawing and painting materials, scissors, adhesive, straw, 'litter', crêpe and tissue paper, reclaimed boxes, tubes, tubs, fabric. Two contrasting shades of dark blue backing paper, sugar paper, yellow, gold and silver paper pieces. White paper and backing for labels, wool in two colours. Copies of the story, books contrasting town and country. (Refer also to the activity on page 79 and to photocopiable sheet 96.)

Preparation

Put up the two shades of blue paper and cut sugar paper into appropriate sizes for different objects. Write or stencil the title 'Town or country?'.

What to do

Talk to the children about what each mouse found different in his or her new environment. Ask the children for a list of things the mice could see in the country and record their responses. Do the same for town scenery.

Now ask the children to draw, paint or make an object for each environment. Explain that they will be put onto the wall. Allow them as much choice as possible, but encourage them to work to a scale that makes the finished display easy to interpret. For example, reclaimed boxes could be used to make a car or could be combined to make town houses or a farm. Some children might choose to do close observational drawings of berries, 'fancy food' or heads of wheat. Encourage the children to refer to the stories – they may like to choose some cats, sunsets and stars which could appear in either environment.

Once the objects have been attractively arranged and labelled on the display board, put up the title question. Then ask the children to help you link each object to 'town' or 'country' using the contrasting wool. There will be a number of items which can be linked to both and which will prompt further discussions. Link the display together with silver, gold and yellow stars and a moon dotted amongst the paintings and models.

Discussion

Help the children remember key features of the town and country scenery from the story. Ask: what could a mouse see in a crowded shopping centre? What could a mouse see in a field of wheat? As they paint, draw or model, support their accuracy by questioning the shape, size, colours and function of what they're recording.

Follow-up activities

▲ Make a display of contrasting town and country toy objects such as cars, buses and tractors, encouraging children to sort them in different ways.
▲ Collect photos of where the children, their friends and family live, sorting them into town or country.

Mice

What you need

Dark blue backing paper, paints, tissue paper, sugar paper, scraps of material and wool, sketching pencils and paper. Real mice to observe. Paper of different types and thicknesses, brown, black and yellow sugar paper.

Preparation

Put up blue backing paper, leaving a strip along the bottom for observational drawings of the real mice. Cut up the sugar paper so that there are two matching sizes for each mouse, and to make brown and yellow steps for Town Mouse's section. (See illustration.)

What to do

Start by letting the children observe your visiting pet mouse quietly in groups. Then ask the children to record details of what the mouse looks like and does, using special sketching pencils and paper. Mount this work carefully to go along the bottom of your display. (See illustration.)

Now use their mouse expertise to ask them to produce a picture showing Town Mouse and Country Mouse relaxing at the end of the day in their own locations. The display should be split so that the mice can be back to back, each surveying their ideal scene.

Divide the children so that two pairs can concentrate on each mouse, painting and then adding material clothes, hats and so on. Use wool strands to weave long fluffy tails. Others can make a green, brown or yellow field, perhaps printing with the side of card. Use different types of twisted paper to create stems for red poppy flowers and heads of corn. Use tissue or crêpe paper for the petals and ears of corn. Show Country Mouse admiring a sunset or twinkling stars. For Town Mouse, use the sugar paper to make giant steps and twisted paper for railings. Decorate with elaborate patterns and cut up squares for the pavement. Add gold and silver artwork and brick printing behind the steps. Label each part of your display.

Discussion

As the children work, discuss the different types of clothes that each mouse would wear. Think about 'mouse perspective' and ask: how big does a flower seem? What would a step look like? Encourage the children to consider why each mouse feels so relaxed and contented in their own homes. How do the children feel when they are in their own home or bedroom?

Follow-up activities

▲ Make a collection of books and toy mice.
▲ Design play equipment for your visiting real mouse and watch what fun it has!

▲ **85**
Starting with story
Animal story activities

Say cheese!

Group size
Four to six children.

What you need
Knife, fork, wooden spoon, rolling pin, mixing bowls, sieve, pastry cutter shapes, grater, baking trays, wire rack, clear plastic film. Aprons, washing up equipment. Ingredients: 225g plain flour, teaspoon salt, teaspoon baking powder, pinch dried mustard, 50g diced chilled butter, 50g grated Red Leicester cheese, 2 tablespoons chilled water (makes at least 30 small shapes).

What to do
Ensure children understand safety and hygiene rules. Set the oven at 190°C (375°F, Gas Mark 5). Sift the dry ingredients into the mixing bowl. Add the diced butter and the finely grated cheese. Show the children how to rub the fat and flour using their fingertips. Continue until the mixture looks like fine bread crumbs. Make a well in the centre and mix the water, a little at a time, quickly and lightly with a blunt knife or wooden spoon. When the mixture leaves the sides cleanly, press together into a ball. Knead together gently with one hand (not for too long.) Wrap this ball in cling film and leave it in the fridge for half an hour while you clear and wash up. Lightly flour a surface and your rolling pins and flatten out your chilled pastry. Roll the pastry out, thinking about creating an even thickness and not letting the pastry get too thin. Use the cutters to form interesting shapes, or mould your own designs lightly by hand. Prick the base of your designs and space out carefully on lightly greased baking trays. Cook in the centre of the oven for 10 to 15 minutes, until golden brown. Leave to cool on wire racks and enjoy the delicious smells.

Discussion
Explore contrasting tactile qualities and ask the children how ingredients are prepared – chopped, sieved, diced or grated – to make mixing them easier. Look at the changes once liquid has been added, noting how important it is to get the quantity right. Talk through rubbing and rolling out techniques with the children.

Follow-up activities
▲ Experiment with different pastry flavourings, such as herbs, spices and garlic.
▲ Contrast sweet and savoury pastry recipes.
▲ Explore other ways of making pastry, resulting in different tastes and appearance.
▲ Find ingredients which change the colour of pastry such as tomato puree, turmeric or chocolate.

Piggy in the middle?

▲Find the odd one out in each row, colour it in.

▲Colour the other two pictures *exactly* the same as each other.

photocopiable
▶ **activities** ◀

Story map

▲Draw arrows to show the route of the three pigs.

▲Draw some pictures of the things that they saw.

Guess it Goldilocks! (P24) and
Pour the porridge (P26)

photocopiable
►activities◄

Size it up!

Goldilocks has messed these things up!

▲Colour in the objects and cut out the card shapes.

▲Put them in order of size.

Starting with story
Animal story activities

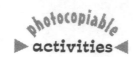

Favourite porridge

▲Fill in the table using ticks.

▲Choose your favourite porridge.

Name of bear _____

Age of bear _____ Paw print

My favourite porridge is _____

Porridge type	Porridge alone	Porridge and salt	Porridge and cheese	Porridge and raisins	Porridge and chocolate
sweet					
sour					
lumpy					
smooth					
like					
don't like					

Hen house hop!

▲Follow each trail to find out who gets Hen's bread bun. Use a different colour for each one.

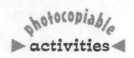

Photocopiable ▶ **activities** ◀

Now and then

▲Sort these pictures into 'now' and 'then'.

▲Put them in order and colour them carefully.

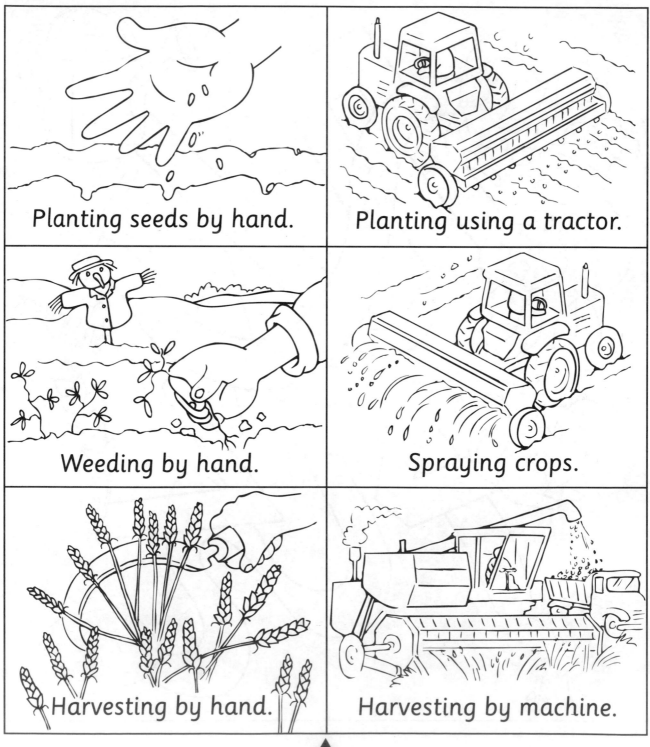

Planting seeds by hand.

Planting using a tractor.

Weeding by hand.

Spraying crops.

Harvesting by hand.

Harvesting by machine.

Goat templates

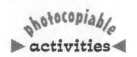
photocopiable
▶ activities ◀

Bridge game

▲Help goat to cross the bridge using a special dice.

Green dots – move forwards.

Red dots – move backwards.   Good luck!

Mouse's journey

▲Find a route for Mouse to get to school. Talk about your ideas before you mark the route onto the map.

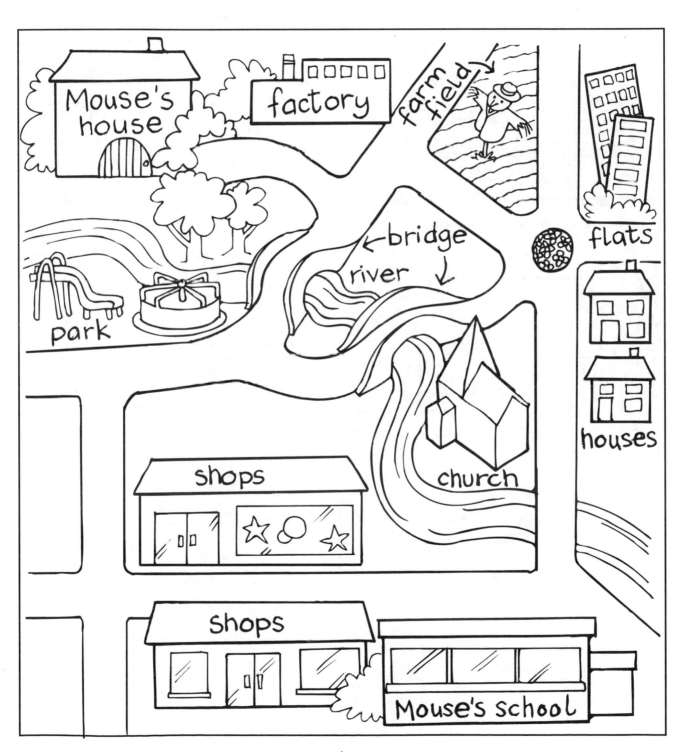

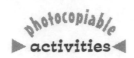
photocopiable ►**activities**◄

Town and country scenes

▲Look at the pictures. Colour them in carefully.

▲Underline the labels for town scenes in red and for country scenes in green.

housing estate

busy road

country house

buses and train station

rural road

farmland

Starting with story
Animal story activities